greek myths
and
legends

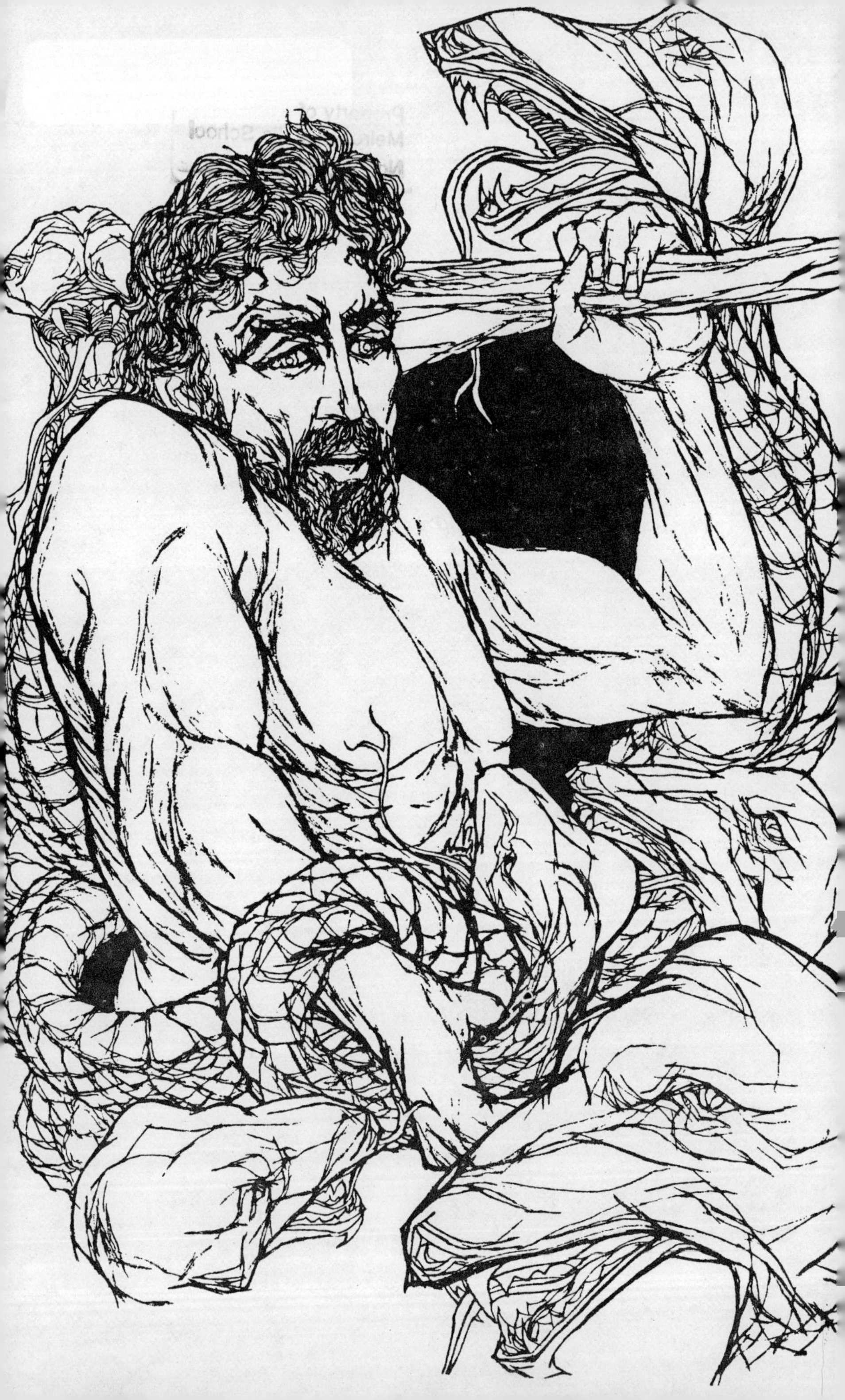

LITERARY HERITAGE
ADVISORY EDITORIAL BOARD

Dora V. Smith
Richard Corbin
John D. Ebbs

Greek myths and Legends

Retold by Eminent Mythologists
Compiled by
JAMES R. SQUIRE
and
BARBARA L. SQUIRE

LITERARY HERITAGE SERIES

THE MACMILLAN COMPANY   NEW YORK
COLLIER-MACMILLAN LIMITED, LONDON

© Copyright The Macmillan Company 1967

All rights reserved. No part of this book may be reproduced or utilized in any form or by any means, electronic or mechanical, including photocopying, recording or by any information storage and retrieval system, without permission in writing from the Publisher.

The editors would like to thank Kitty, Kevin, and David for reading and enjoying the myths, and would like to express their appreciation to Miss Lynn Chilton and Miss Judith Rothstein for their assistance in the preparation of *Greek Myths and Legends*.

ACKNOWLEDGMENTS

For permission to use material in this book grateful acknowledgment is made to the following:

The Dial Press, Inc.: For "The Golden Fleece" reprinted from *Stories of the Gods and Heroes* by Sally Benson; copyright 1940 by Sally Benson: and used with the permission of the publishers, The Dial Press, Inc.

Farrar, Straus and Giroux, Inc. and MacGibbon and Kee Ltd.: For "The Labours of Hercules" reprinted from *Men and Gods* by Rex Warner by permission of Farrar, Straus and Giroux, Inc. and MacGibbon and Kee Ltd. All rights reserved.

George G. Harrap & Co. Ltd.: For "Odysseus and the Cyclops" from *The Children's Homer* by Padraic Colum; © 1918, 1946. By permission of George G. Harrap & Co. Ltd.

Horno N. V., and Cassell and Co.: For "The Palace of Olympus" slightly amended from *Greek Gods and Heroes* (English title *Myths of Ancient Greece*) by Robert Graves; © 1961 International Authors N. V., and "Paris and Queen Helen," "Achilles Avenges Patroclus," and "The Wooden Horse" slightly amended from *The Siege and Fall of Troy* by Robert Graves; © 1962 International Authors N. V., published by Doubleday & Co., Inc., and Cassell and Co. Ltd. Also by permission of A. P. Watt and Son.

Houghton Mifflin Company: For "The Trickery of Hermes," "The Loves of Apollo," and "Phaethon, Son of Apollo" reprinted from *Greek Myths* by Olivia Coolidge. Copyright 1949, by Olivia E. Coolidge. Reprinted by the permission of the publisher, Houghton Mifflin Company. For "The Pomegranate Seeds" and "The Gorgon's Head" from *A Wonder Book and Tanglewood Tales for Girls and Boys* by Nathaniel Hawthorne; © 1898.

J. B. Lippincott Company: For "Echo and Narcissus," and "Arachne" from *Tales from Greek Mythology* by Katharine Pyle; © 1928, 1955 by Walter Pyle. Published by J. B. Lippincott Company. By permission of J. B. Lippincott Company.

Little, Brown and Company: For "Ceyx and Alcyone" from *Mythology* by Edith Hamilton; copyright 1940, 1942 by Edith Hamilton. By permission of Little, Brown and Company.

The Macmillan Company: For "Odysseus and the Cyclops" pp. 156-167. Adapted with the permission of The Macmillan Company from *The Children's Homer* by Padraic Colum; copyright 1918 by The Macmillan Company. Renewed 1946 by Padraic Colum and Willy Pogany. For "How Theseus Slew the Devourers of Men" and "How Theseus Slew the Minotaur" pp. 178-189, adapted with the permission of The Macmillan Company from *Tales of the Heroes* by Charles Kingsley.

Penguin Books Ltd.: For "The Story of Prometheus" from *Heroes of Greece and Troy* by Roger L. Green; copyright 1961. By permission of Penguin Books Ltd.

Illustrations by Kenneth Longtemps

The Macmillan Company, New York
Collier-Macmillan Canada, Ltd., Toronto, Ontario
Printed in the United States of America
ISBN 0-02-254540-9
14 15 16 17 18 19   99 98 97

contents

Reading About the Myths and Legends of Greece   2

Section I: Stories of the Gods

THE PALACE OF OLYMPUS	*Robert Graves*	7
THE STORY OF PROMETHEUS	*Roger L. Green*	22
THE TRICKERY OF HERMES	*Olivia Coolidge*	34
THE LOVES OF APOLLO	*Olivia Coolidge*	40
PHAETHON, SON OF APOLLO	*Olivia Coolidge*	45
ECHO AND NARCISSUS	*Katharine Pyle*	54
ARACHNE	*Katharine Pyle*	59
CEYX AND ALCYONE	*Edith Hamilton*	67
THE POMEGRANATE SEEDS	*Nathaniel Hawthorne*	73

Section II: Adventures of Heroes

THE GOLDEN FLEECE	*Sally Benson*	121
THESEUS AND THE MINOTAUR	*Charles Kingsley*	133
THE LABOURS OF HERCULES	*Rex Warner*	146
PERSEUS	*Nathaniel Hawthorne*	161
ODYSSEUS AND POLYPHEMUS	*Padraic Colum*	195

Section III: Tales of the Trojan War

PARIS AND QUEEN HELEN	*Robert Graves*	209
ACHILLES AVENGES PATROCLUS	*Robert Graves*	220
THE WOODEN HORSE	*Robert Graves*	234

Glossary   250

Reading about the Myths and Legends of Greece

THOUSANDS of years ago when man lived in caves he found the world awesome and baffling. He looked at the sky during a storm. Why did it rain? What caused flashes across the heavens? He listened. What made the rumbling noises?

Man began to make up stories to answer his questions about the world around him. In these stories, he tried to explain the great windstorms, the sun and the moon, the existence of men and animals. Man imagined that beings more powerful than himself must be responsible for the marvels of nature. So he created mighty gods and goddesses. He thought these gods and goddesses caused the mysterious happenings of nature that puzzled him. These stories that explained the causes of natural phenomena are called myths. Myths became the basis of early science.

Early man also told stories which we call legends. Legends are stories that were originally based on historical happenings. But the historical events became exaggerated as the legends were passed down through the years, from father to son to grandson.

Some legends tell about courageous men who fought vicious monsters. They arose something like this. The triumphant hero who had just slaughtered a wild animal described the animal's growls and tusks and claws to his family and friends. Another person who told the story exaggerated, and said the ferocious animal had two heads. People enjoyed hearing about the two-headed monster so much that another person told the same story about a three-headed monster. The story became more and more exciting, as it was told and retold.

Other legends grew out of great wars. The heroes and battles achieved legendary stature after hundreds of years of retellings. The stories of the Trojan War, a ten-year struggle that took place about twelve hundred years B.C., are legendary stories.

Early people told and retold the stories about gods and goddesses and heroes for hundreds of years. Between two and three thousand years ago, Homer and other Greek poets began to write the stories down. When Rome conquered Greece in the second century B.C., the Roman soldiers listened to Greek captives tell the stories. They enjoyed the stories so much that they took them home to Rome and told them in Latin. Much later, British and then American writers began to retell the stories in English.

Myths and legends are the earliest stories recorded by people. Many are available today only as fragments. Snatches have been found on parts of wall paintings in the ruins of Greek cities. Scholars have discovered information from bits of papyrus and parchment and from detail on Greek sculpture.

The versions of the myths and legends in this book are told by British and American mythologists. These British and American mythologists have used original Greek sources for their stories; but, of course, they have retold the stories in English.

Although the Greek myths and legends are thousands of years old, people still enjoy reading them today.

stories of the gods

section 1

The people of ancient Greece believed in many gods and goddesses. They thought gods and goddesses inhabited the underworld, the sea, land, and the heavens.

The Greeks were the first people to create gods in their own image. These gods looked like men and had many of the traits and feelings of men—anger, love, fear, strength, jealousy, loyalty—but they always had them in large godly proportions. The Greek people thought the gods watched over them—rewarding the good men and punishing the bad. Sometimes the Greeks feared the gods and offered sacrifices to appease them. Sometimes they prayed to gods for help. Other times they laughed at them and loved them.

Believing in the gods made the Greeks feel more secure in a puzzling world. They could understand a sea storm if they thought an angry god had caused it. They could explain the failure of their crops by saying the gods were punishing man for some evil he had done. They could attribute pleasant weather to the kindness of a god. With these explanations, the Greeks could cope with a world which otherwise seemed too strange, too fearful, and too uncertain.

The Greeks loved to listen to stories about their gods. These stories explained happenings in nature and told of marvelous adventures. Often there were several versions of the same story. Sometimes the versions were quite similar; sometimes they were contradictory. Now you will read some of the myths about the gods and goddesses.

The twelve major gods and goddesses of Greece were a spirited family who lived on Mt. Olympus. Like many large families they joked, quarreled, and teased each other; often they were quite rowdy. Whether the gods were angry or content, serious or comical, their ideas and antics showed that they were unique individuals.

BY ROBERT GRAVES

the palace of olympus

The twelve most important gods and goddesses of ancient Greece, called the Olympians, belonged to the same large, quarrelsome family. Though thinking little of the smaller, old-fashioned gods over whom they ruled, they thought even less of mortals. All the Olympians lived together in an enormous palace, set well above the usual level of clouds at the top of Mount Olympus,* the highest mountain in Greece. Great walls, too steep for climbing, protected the Palace. The Olympians' masons, gigantic one-eyed Cyclopes,* had built them on much the same plan as royal palaces on earth.

At the southern end, just behind the Council Hall, and looking towards the famous Greek cities of Athens, Thebes,* Sparta, Corinth, Argos, and Mycenae,* were the private apartments of King Zeus,* the

*Olympus (ō-lim′-pəs)   *Mycenae (mī-sē′-nē)   7
*Cyclopes (sī′-klō-pēz) *Zeus (Zōos)
*Thebes (thēbz)

Father-god, and Queen Hera,* the Mother-goddess. The northern end of the palace, looking across the valley of Tempe* towards the wild hills of Macedonia, consisted of the kitchen, banqueting hall, armoury, workshops, and servants' quarters. In between came a square court, open to the sky, with covered cloisters and private rooms on each side, belonging to the other five Olympian gods and the other five Olympian goddesses. Beyond the kitchen and servants' quarters stood cottages for smaller gods, sheds for chariots, stables for horses, kennels for hounds, and a sort of zoo where the Olympians kept their sacred animals. These included a bear, a lion, a peacock, an eagle, tigers, stags, a cow, a crane, snakes, a wild boar, white bulls, a wild cat, mice, swans, herons, an owl, a tortoise, and a tank full of fish.

In the Council Hall the Olympians met at times to discuss mortal affairs—such as which army on earth should be allowed to win a war, and whether they ought to punish some king or queen who had been behaving proudly or disgustingly. But for the most part they were too busy with their own quarrels and lawsuits to take much notice of mortal affairs.

King Zeus had an enormous throne of polished black Egyptian marble, decorated in gold. Seven steps led up to it, each of them enamelled with one of the seven colours of the rainbow. A bright blue covering above showed that the whole sky belonged to Zeus alone; and on the right arm of his throne perched a ruby-eyed golden eagle clutching jagged strips of pure tin, which meant that Zeus could kill whatever enemies he pleased by throwing a thunderbolt of forked lightning at them.

*Hera (hêr'-ə)   *Tempe (tem'-pi)

A purple ram's fleece covered the cold seat. Zeus used it for magical rain-making in times of drought. He was a strong, brave, stupid, noisy, violent, conceited god, and always on the watch lest his family should try to get rid of him; having once himself got rid of his wicked, idle, cannibalistic father Cronus,* King of the Titans* and Titanesses. The Olympians could not die, but Zeus, with the help of his two elder brothers, Hades* and Poseidon,* had banished Cronus to a distant island in the Atlantic—perhaps the Azores, perhaps Torrey Island, off the coast of Ireland. Zeus, Hades, and Poseidon then drew lots for the three parts of Cronus's kingdom. Zeus won the sky; Poseidon, the sea; Hades, the Underworld; they shared the earth between them. One of Zeus's emblems was the eagle; another was the woodpecker.

Queen Hera had an ivory throne, with three crystal steps leading up to it. Golden cuckoos and willow leaves decorated the back, and a full moon hung above it. Hera sat on a white cowskin, which she sometimes used for rain-making magic if Zeus could not be bothered to stop a drought. She disliked being Zeus's wife, because he was frequently marrying mortal women and saying, with a sneer, that these marriages did not count—his brides would soon grow ugly and die; but she was his Queen, and perpetually young and beautiful.

When first asked to marry him, Hera had refused; and had gone on refusing every year for three hundred years. But one springtime Zeus disguised himself as a poor cuckoo caught in a thunderstorm, and tapped at her window. Hera, not seeing through his disguise, let the cuckoo in, stroked his wet feathers, and whispered:

---

*Cronus (krō'-nəs)   *Hades (hā'-dēz)
*Titan (tī'-tən)   *Poseidon (pō-sī'-d'n)

'Poor bird, I love you.' At once, Zeus changed back again into his true shape, and said: 'Now you must marry me!' After this, however badly Zeus behaved, Hera felt obliged to set a good example to gods and goddesses and mortals, as the Mother of Heaven. Her emblem was the cow, the most motherly of animals; but, not wishing to be thought as plain-looking and placid as a cow, she also used the peacock and the lion.

These two thrones faced down the Council Hall towards the door leading into the open courtyard. Along the sides of the hall stood ten other thrones—for five goddesses on Hera's side, for five gods on Zeus's.

Poseidon, god of the seas and rivers, had the second-largest throne. It was of grey-green white-streaked marble, ornamented with coral, gold, and mother-of-pearl. The arms were carved in the shape of sea-beasts, and Poseidon sat on sealskin. For his help in banishing Cronus and the Titans, Zeus had married him to Amphitrite,* the former Sea-goddess, and allowed him to take over all her titles. Though Poseidon hated to be less important than his younger brother, and always went about scowling, he feared Zeus's thunderbolt. His only weapon was a trident, with which he could stir up the sea and so wreck ships; but Zeus never travelled by ship. When Poseidon felt even crosser than usual, he would drive away in his chariot to a palace under the waves, near the island of Euboea,* and there let his rage cool. As his emblem Poseidon chose the horse, an animal which he pretended to have created. Large waves are still called 'white horses' because of this.

Opposite Poseidon sat his sister Demeter,* goddess of all useful fruits, grasses, and grains. Her throne of

*Amphitrite (am'-fə-trī'-ti)   *Demeter (di-mē'-tēr)
*Euboea (ū-bē'-ə)

bright green malachite was ornamented with ears of barley in gold, and little golden pigs for luck. Demeter seldom smiled, except when her daughter Persephone*—unhappily married to the hateful Hades, God of the Dead—came to visit her once a year. Demeter's emblem was the poppy, which grows red as blood among the barley.

Next to Poseidon sat Hephaestus,* a son of Zeus and Hera. Being the god of goldsmiths, jewellers, blacksmiths, masons, and carpenters, he had built all these thrones himself, and made his own a masterpiece of every different metal and precious stone to be found. The seat could swivel about, the arms could move up and down, and the whole throne rolled along automatically wherever he wished, like the three-legged golden tables in his workshop. Hephaestus had hobbled ever since birth, when Zeus roared at Hera: 'A brat as weak as this is unworthy of me!'—and threw him far out over the walls of Olympus. In his fall Hephaestus broke a leg so badly that he had to wear a golden leg-iron. He kept a country house on Lemnos, the island where he had struck earth; and his emblem was the quail, a bird that does a hobbling dance in springtime.

Opposite Hephaestus sat Athene,* Goddess of Wisdom, who first taught him how to handle tools, and knew more than anyone else about pottery, weaving, and all useful arts. Her silver throne had golden basketwork at the back and sides, and a crown of violets, made from blue lapis lazuli, set above it. Its arms ended in grinning Gorgons' heads. Athene, wise though she was, did not know the names of her parents. Poseidon claimed her as his daughter by a marriage with an African goddess

*Persephone (pēr-sef'-ə-ni)   *Athena (ə-thē'-nə)
*Hephaestus (hi-fes'-təs)

called Libya. It is true that, as a child, she had been found wandering in a goatskin by the shores of a Libyan lake; but rather than admit herself the daughter of Poseidon, whom she thought very stupid, she allowed Zeus to pretend she was his. Zeus announced that one day, overcome by a fearful headache, he had howled aloud like a thousand wolves hunting in a pack. Hephaestus, he said, then ran up with an axe and kindly split open his skull, and out sprang Athene, dressed in full armour. Athene was also a Battle-goddess, yet never went to war unless forced—being too sensible to pick quarrels—and when she fought, always won. She chose the wise owl as her emblem; and she had a town house at Athens.

Next to Athene sat Aphrodite,* Goddess of Love and Beauty. Nobody knew who her parents were, either. The South Wind said that he had once seen her floating in a scallop shell off the island of Cythera,* and steered her gently ashore. She may have been a daughter of Amphitrite by a smaller god named Triton, who used to blow roaring blasts on a conch, or perhaps by old Cronus. Amphitrite refused to say a word on the subject. Aphrodite's throne was silver, inlaid with beryls and aquamarines, the back shaped like a scallop shell, the seat made of swan's down, and under her feet lay a golden mat—an embroidery of golden bees, apples, and sparrows. Aphrodite had a magic girdle, which she would wear whenever she wanted to make anyone love her madly. To keep Aphrodite out of mischief, Zeus decided that she needed a hard-working, decent husband; and naturally chose his son Hephaestus. Aphrodite's emblem

*Aphrodite (af'-rə-dī'-ti)   *Cythera (si'-thir-ə)

was the dove, and she would visit Paphos, in Cyprus,* once a year to swim in the sea, for good luck.

Opposite Aphrodite sat Ares,* Hephaestus's tall, handsome, boastful, cruel brother, who loved fighting for its own sake. Ares and Aphrodite were continually holding hands and giggling in corners, which made Hephaestus jealous. Yet if he ever complained to the Council, Zeus would laugh at him, saying: 'Fool, why did you give your wife that magic girdle? Can you blame your brother if he falls in love with her when she wears it?' Ares's throne was built of brass, strong and ugly—those huge brass knobs in the shape of skulls, and that cushion-cover of human skin! Ares had no manners, no learning, and the worst of taste; yet Aphrodite thought him wonderful. His emblems were a wild boar and a bloodstained spear. He kept a country house among the rough woods of Thrace.*

Next to Ares sat Apollo,* the god of music, poetry, medicine, archery, and young unmarried men—Zeus's son by Leto, one of the smaller goddesses, whom he married to annoy Hera. Apollo rebelled against his father once or twice, but got well punished each time, and learned to behave more sensibly. His highly polished golden throne had magical inscriptions carved all over it, a back shaped like a lyre, and a python skin to sit on. Above hung a golden sun-disk with twenty-one rays shaped like arrows, because he pretended to manage the Sun. Apollo's emblem was a mouse; mice were supposed to know the secrets of earth, and tell them to him. (He preferred white mice to ordinary ones; most boys still do.) Apollo married several mortal wives at different times.

*Cyprus (sī'-prəs)   *Thrace (thrās)
*Ares (âr'-ēz)   *Apollo (ə-pol'-ō)

Once he chased a girl named Daphne,* who cried out for help to Mother Earth and got turned into a laurel tree before he could catch and kiss her. Apollo owned a splendid house at Delphi on the top of Mount Parnassus, built around the famous oracle which he stole from Mother Earth, Zeus's grandmother.

Opposite Apollo sat his twin-sister, Artemis,* goddess of hunting and of unmarried girls, from whom he had learned medicine and archery. Her throne was of pure silver, with a wolfskin to sit on, and the back shaped like two date palms, one on each side of a new-moon boat. Artemis hated the idea of marriage, although she kindly took care of mothers when their babies were born. She much preferred hunting, fishing, and swimming in moonlit mountain pools. If any mortal happened to see her without clothes, she used to change him into a stag and hunt him to death. She chose as her emblem the she-bear, the most dangerous of all wild animals in Greece.

Last in the row of gods sat Hermes,* Zeus's son by a smaller goddess named Maia,* after whom the month of May is called. Hermes, the god of merchants, bankers, thieves, fortune-tellers, and heralds, was born in Arcadia.* His throne was cut out of a single piece of solid grey rock, with arms shaped like rams' heads, and a goatskin for the seat. On its back he had carved a swastika, this being the shape of a fire-making machine invented by him—the fire-drill. Until then, housewives used to borrow glowing pieces of charcoal from their neighbours. Hermes also invented the alphabet; and one of his emblems was the crane, because cranes fly in a V—the first letter he wrote. Another of Hermes's em-

*Daphne (daf'-ni)   *Maia (mā'-yə)
*Artemis (är'-tə-mis)   *Arcadia (är'-kā'-di-ə)
*Hermes (hūr'-mēz)

blems was a peeled hazel stick, which he carried as the Messenger of the Olympians: white ribbons dangled from it, which foolish people often mistook for snakes.

Last in the row of goddesses sat Zeus's eldest sister, Hestia,* Goddess of the Home, on a plain, uncarved, wooden throne, and a plain cushion woven of undyed wool. Hestia, the kindest and most peaceable of all the Olympians, hated the continual family quarrels, and never troubled to choose any particular emblem of her own. She used to tend the charcoal hearth in the middle of the Council Hall.

That made six gods and six goddesses. But one day Zeus announced that Dionysus,* his son by a mortal woman named Semele,* had invented wine, and must be given a seat in the Council. Thirteen Olympians would have been an unlucky number; so Hestia offered him her seat, just to keep the peace. Now there were seven gods and five goddesses; an unjust state of affairs because, when questions about women had to be discussed, the gods outvoted the goddesses. Dionysus's throne was gold-plated fir wood, ornamented with bunches of grapes carved in amethyst (a violet-coloured stone), snakes carved in serpentine (a stone with many markings), and various horned animals besides, carved in onyx (a black and white stone), sard (a dark red stone), jade (a dark green stone), and carnelian (a pink stone). He took the tiger for his emblem, having once visited India at the head of an army and brought tigers back as souvenirs.

In a room behind the kitchen sat the Three Fates, named Clotho,* Lachesis,* and Atropos.* They were the oldest goddesses in existence, too old for anybody to re-

*Hestia (hes′-ti-ə)   *Clotho (klō′-thō)
*Dionysus (dī′-ə-nī′-səs)   *Lachesis (lak′-ə-sis)
*Semele (sem′-ə-li)   *Atropos (at′-rə-pōs′)

15

member where they came from. The Fates decided how long each mortal should live: spinning a linen thread, to measure exactly so many inches and feet for months and years, and then snipping it off with a pair of shears. They also knew, but seldom revealed, what would be the fate of each Olympian god. Even Zeus feared them for that reason.

The Olympians drank nectar, a sweet drink made from fermented honey; and ate ambrosia, said to be an uncooked mixture of honey, water, fruit, olive oil, cheese, and barley—though this may be doubted. Some claim that certain speckled mushrooms were the true food of the Olympians, created whenever Zeus's thunderbolt struck the earth; and that this kept them immortal. Because the Olympians also loved the smell, though not the taste, of roast beef and mutton, mortals used to sacrifice sheep and cattle to them, afterwards eating the meat themselves.

TALKING ABOUT THE STORY

1. The ancient Greeks were full of questions when they looked at the world. Why were leaves green? Why did waterfalls go down instead of up? How could birds fly?

    Zeus's thunderbolt explained something in nature. What?

    How did stories of Poseidon's activities answer questions about nature?

Can you think of any other gods who had power in nature? Who were they and what aspects of nature could they affect?

2. The gods and goddesses had good and bad qualities. Which goddesses might have assisted housewives? How? How were other Olympians helpful or kind?

   Some Olympians had terrible tempers. Which ones? How did they "let off steam"? What other undesirable qualities could you see in the gods?

   Do these imperfections make the gods seem more human or less human? Why?

3. Each of the following animals was associated with a particular god or goddess: eagle, peacock, owl, dove. To whom was each animal linked? What qualities does each of these creatures suggest in the modern world? Do you see any connection between these qualities and the god associated with each animal?

4. Could you visualize the thrones in the Palace at Olympus? Each one just suited the god who sat in it.

   Suppose that you could paint Hephaestus's throne. What colors would you use? Why? How would you paint Aphrodite's throne? Ares's? Demeter's? the others?

5. In the story you have read, Robert Graves told about the appearance, interests, and habits of the gods and goddesses. Suppose you could go back to early Greece. Would you be able to recognize Olympians who were visiting earth? How?

6. As you were reading, you may have noticed that the author had quite a good time poking fun at the gods. Look back through "The Palace of Olympus" and see if you can find passages that Robert Graves might have chuckled over as he wrote.

GREEK CUSTOMS LIVE ON

The Olympic Games

The Greeks worshipped physical fitness. Every four years men entered the Olympic Games, a sports festival honoring Zeus in which great athletes from all over Greece competed.

The Games opened with sacrifices of animals. Then the athletes swore to abide by the rules and the judges promised to be fair. Next there was a parade around the stadium. The events were announced by trumpet blasts. The winners received crowns of olive and branches of palm. At dusk the victors treated their friends and relatives to a supper at which poets, writers, and philosophers could present their works.

The first Olympic Games were held about 776 B.C. The first festival lasted for just one day and consisted of only the 210-yard dash. Gradually, as longer races, wrestling, broad jumping, spear throwing, and discus hurling were added, the games grew to a five-day celebration.

The Roman Emperor Theodosius stopped the Olympic Games in 394 A.D. They were not held again until fifteen hundred years later. Baron Pierre de Coubertin, a French sports enthusiast, revived them in 1896. Now the Olympic Games last for two weeks and include athletes from many countries.

WORDS FROM MYTHOLOGY

Mortal and Immortal

Any animal that can die is *mortal*. Human beings are sometimes called *mortals*. What do you suppose a *mortal* wound would be?

The gods are *immortals;* they do not die. Sometimes poets, athletes, musicians, or soldiers reach *immortality* through their achievements. Even though the men themselves die, their fame "lives on." Can you name any men who have achieved *immortality*? Do you know of any living men whose contributions may make them *immortal*?

IDEAS FOR WRITING

1. Gods and goddesses often visited families on earth. Suppose a god or goddess visited your home town and you offered to show him around. What kind of tour would you plan? Write a composition about the tour and the reactions of the god.

2. If you could invite two of the Olympians to dinner, which ones would you select? What would the menu be? What would the decorations be? How might the conversation go? Write a description of the dinner party.

the gods and goddesses have greek names and latin names

When legions of Roman soldiers conquered Greece during the second century B.C., they overran Greek cities and collected statues to take back to Rome. They listened to Greek captives tell myths about the gods and goddesses and were reminded of their own gods and goddesses. They liked the stories so much that when they returned to Rome, they told them in Latin to family and friends. They kept the Latin names their gods already had.

On the opposite page is a chart of the gods and goddesses of Greece and Rome. Look at the names on the chart. Compare the Latin (Roman) names with the Greek names. Since you have already read "The Palace of Olympus," you will recognize the Greek names. Which set of names was more familiar to you before you started reading this book? Can you think of things that have been named after the gods? Can you think of words that have been formed from the names of gods?

The gods and goddesses "live on" today in statues, trademarks, medals, and seals. For example, the winged foot of Hermes appears on a Boy Scout merit badge. Other places where you can look for signs of the gods are newspapers, magazines, decorations on buildings and labels on products in your supermarket. See how many traces of the gods and goddesses you can find.

As you read this book, you will notice that the mythologists who retell myths and legends use either Greek or Latin names for the gods. This is not the only way in which the stories differ. The writing of the mythologists varies, depending on what they want to tell and whom they wish to read the stories. Some authors emphasize action; others, conversation; others, description.

The Gods and Goddesses of Greece and Rome

Greek Name		Latin Name
Zeus	King of the Gods	Jupiter
Hera	Queen of the Gods	Juno
Poseidon	God of the Seas	Neptune
Demeter	Goddess of Agriculture	Ceres
Hades	God of the Underworld	Pluto
Athena	Goddess of Wisdom and Handicrafts	Minerva
Hermes	Messenger of the Gods and God of Thieves	Mercury
Aphrodite	Goddess of Love and Beauty	Venus
Apollo	God of the Sun and Music	Apollo
Ares	God of War	Mars
Artemis	Goddess of the Hunt and the Moon	Diana
Hephaestus	God of Fire and the Forge	Vulcan
Hestia	Goddess of the Home	Vesta
Dionysus	God of Wine	Bacchus

Prometheus was one of the Titans, the giant gods who had ruled the world before Zeus overthrew them. When Zeus fought for power on Mount Olympus, Prometheus helped him defeat the other Titans. Later, he helped Zeus form human beings out of clay. But when Prometheus decided to disobey the king of the gods, he paid a terrible price for his decision.

BY ROGER L. GREEN

the story of prometheus

After he had formed men out of the clay of Panopeus,* and they had received the breath of life from Zeus, Prometheus* set to work to make them something more than mere living images of the gods. For man as first created was little better than the beasts, a poor creature, who did not know how to think or how to use the things which he saw and felt round about him. He lived in caves, ate herbs and raw meat: and when he was wounded or hurt, he died because he knew nothing of medicine or surgery.

But Prometheus, the good and kind, taught men all the arts and crafts of life. He taught them how to build houses and make tools; how to plough the earth and sow the corn, how to reap it when it had grown, to thresh out the bright grains and grind them between flat stones. He showed them how to

*Panopeus (pan-o'-pē-əs)   *Prometheus (prə-mē'-thūs)

catch and tame some of the wild creatures: the dog to guard their houses and go hunting with them; the horse to draw their chariots, and the ox to pull the plough; the sheep to yield wool, and the goats milk which might be made into cheese.

It is said that Prometheus also gave men the power of speech, taught them the names of all things and even how to write and read.

But it was slow work, since fire, the greatest aid, was missing. Without it meat must still be eaten raw, and tools could be made only of stone and wood; bread could not be baked, and houses could not be warmed in winter.

Prometheus looked up at the sun, coursing across the sky in the golden chariot which Helios* drove, and he sighed deeply. For he could read the future, and, though much of it remained dark to him, what he could see he knew would surely happen.

Then he called to him his brother Epimetheus,* who was as foolish, thoughtless, and improvident as Prometheus was wise, thoughtful, and foresighted.

'My brother,' he said, 'you have helped me so far, and now you live as a man among men to carry on my work. You know how well I love the men whom we have made and taught—and yet you, who see only the outward aspect of everything, do not realize how deep such a love as mine can be. Listen! I must give fire to mankind, the last and greatest of gifts. But if I do so, I shall incur the terrible wrath of Zeus. . . . Yet even that I will endure—for so it is ordained. But I beg you to guard mankind to the best of your power, and to be very careful when I am no longer with you. Above all things, beware of any gift from Zeus.'

*Helios (hē'-li-os')   *Epimetheus (ep'-ə-mē'-thŭs)

Then Prometheus bade farewell to his brother, and set out for Olympus, carrying with him the stalk of a fennel plant, as long as a staff and hard as wood, but hollow and filled with a white pith which would burn slowly and steadily like the wick of a candle.

At the foot of Olympus he was met by Athena, the Immortal daughter of Zeus, Lady of Wisdom, who had helped Prometheus in his labours for mankind. Athena was always friendly to Prometheus, and interested in his work for mankind; and so when she knew that he had decided to give men fire, she led him by the secret paths to the summit of Olympus.

As day drew to an end, Helios drove up in his shining chariot, and Prometheus, hiding by the gateway, needed but to stretch out his fennel-stalk and touch the golden wheel. Then, the precious spark concealed under his cloak, he hastened down the mountain side, and away into a deep valley of Arcadia where he heaped up a pile of wood and kindled it.

The first people upon earth to see the wonderful new gift of fire were the wild satyrs* who dwelt in the lonely valleys. Slowly and shyly they gathered round the edge of the glade in which Prometheus had lighted the first camp-fire; and gradually they drew nearer and nearer.

'Oh the lovely thing!' they cried as they felt the warmth. 'How beautifully it dances; how warm, and gentle, and comforting this creature is!'

'Oh, how I love it!' cried Silenus.* 'It shall be mine, mine! See, I will kiss the lovely creature, to prove it!'

With that he knelt down and tried to kiss the tallest and brightest tongue of flame. The look on his face was

*satyrs (sat′-erz)   *Silenus (sī-lē′-nus)

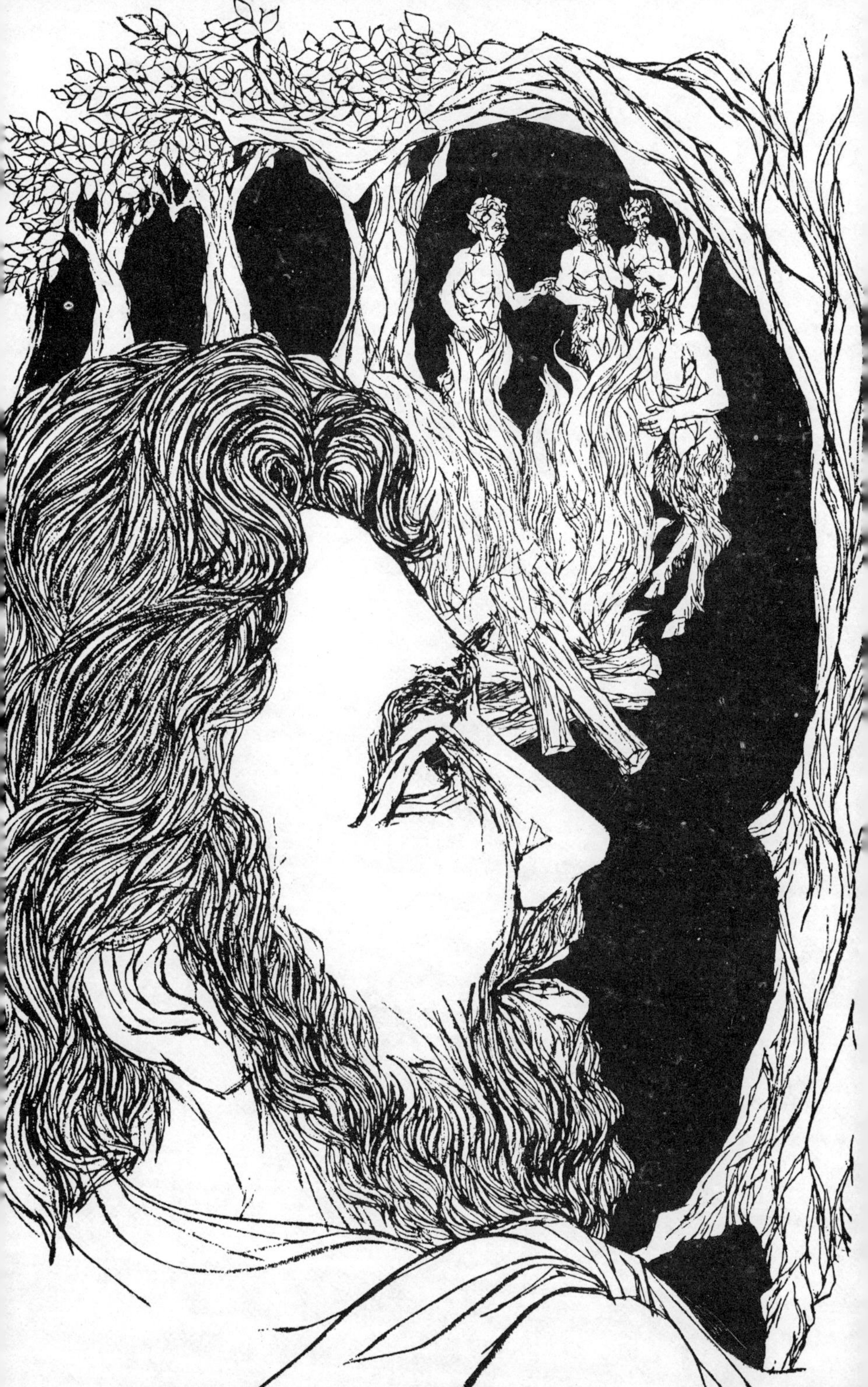

so comical as the flame scorched him and burnt his beard, that Prometheus sat back and roared with laughter.

But he had more serious work in hand, and when day dawned he began to teach men the uses of fire. He showed them how to cook meat and bake bread; how to make bronze and smelt iron; how to hammer the hot metals into swords and ploughshares and all the other cunning crafts of the smith and the metal-worker.

Now that fire had come upon the Earth, it could be kindled there whenever it was needed. So Prometheus, with the help of Hermes, invented rubbing-sticks and taught men which woods to use and how to twirl the hard piece in the soft until fire was kindled by the friction.

So mankind came into its true inheritance: cities began to grow up, and men to practise all the arts and crafts for which Greece was soon to become famous.

But Zeus, as soon as he became aware that his command had been disobeyed and the gift which he withheld had been stolen and given to men, summoned Prometheus before him.

'Titan!' he cried fiercely. 'You have disobeyed me! What is there to prevent me from casting you down into Tartarus* with your brethren, and destroying these vile insects, these men, to whom you have given gifts reserved for the Immortals alone?'

'Lord Zeus,' answered Prometheus quietly, 'I know what is to come, and how cruelly you will punish me for all I have done. But there are two things you cannot do: no Immortal may take away the gift an Immortal has once given—so you will not deprive men of fire now that I have made it theirs. And I am certain that you will not

*Tartarus (tär'-tə-rəs)

destroy mankind, when I tell you that a man—your son, born of a mortal woman—will save you and all of you who dwell in Olympus in that future day when Earth will bring forth the Giants, meaning to be revenged for the overthrow of the Titans. This I tell you, and you know that my words are true: no Immortal will be able to slay a Giant, but a man will slay them, if he be strong and brave enough. And I will tell you this also: at a certain time in the future you may fall as your father fell.'

Then the wrath of Zeus was terrible. In a voice of thunder he bade his son Hephaestus, the Immortal whose skill was in the working of metals, take Prometheus and bind him with fetters of brass to the great mountain of Caucasus* on the eastern edge of the world.

'There you shall lie,' he cried in his cruel rage, 'for ever and ever as a punishment for your daring and disobedience. The snows of winter will freeze you, and the summer sun will burn you: and your fate shall be a warning to all who would disobey!'

Then sorrowfully Hephaestus took Prometheus, and at his command his two servants, the demons Might and Force, chained him to the rock with fetters that he could not break.

But as Hephaestus was about to leave him there, Prometheus said:

'Zeus, that cruel tyrant, will fall as Cronos fell, unless he can find out how to avert his doom. And how to do that, I alone know!'

Hephaestus reported these words, and Hermes was sent to offer Prometheus his freedom if he would tell the secret.

*Caucasus (kô'-kə-səs)

'If you do not at once disclose what you know,' said Hermes, 'Zeus will torture you until you do so. He will send a fierce eagle who will visit you every day and devour your liver: and every night your liver will grow again so that next day your agonies may be repeated.'

Still Prometheus would not say how Zeus could avoid the fate which hung over him, and, though the eagle did as Zeus had threatened, still he would not tell. But at times his screams echoed over the haunted cliffs and chasms of Caucasus, so that none dared to approach.

Meanwhile Zeus, a prey to fears for the future, and still made cruel by terror, sought how he might plague mankind so that the gift of fire might not make them too happy.

Now at first men had full knowledge of their own future, and Zeus, not knowing that Prometheus, with his great foresight, had taken this power from them, decided to make them immortal also, so that when he had worked his will on them and set free sin and care in the world, they might go mad with terror knowing the sorrows and sufferings which lay in store for them.

He went cunningly to work, visiting men in disguise and asking who had given them the gift of fire.

And men betrayed their benefactor, Prometheus, with cruel thoughtlessness. This gave Zeus his excuse.

'I will reward you,' he said, 'for telling me what I wanted to know, by giving you a jar of nectar, the drink of the Immortals, which keeps them for ever young.'

The men who received this precious gift were overjoyed; but with the usual folly and laziness of mankind, they put it on the back of a donkey and drove it before them towards a place where they meant to keep it in safety. Presently they came to a spring of clear water bubbling from the rock, and when they had refreshed themselves, they sat down to eat at a little distance, leaving the donkey to graze nearby.

Soon the donkey felt thirsty too, and went over to the spring for a drink. But now there was a cunning snake guarding it, who spoke to the donkey with crafty words.

'If you touch my spring, I will bite you, and you will die in agony from the poison.'

'I am dying already—of thirst,' protested the donkey. 'So please let me drink a little of the cool spring water.'

'Well,' said the guileful serpent, 'I'll make a bargain with you. Give me the wine in the jar on your back. It's warm, and nasty, and donkeys don't like wine, anyway. If you give it to me, I'll let you drink as much water from my cool, refreshing spring as you please.'

'Agreed,' cried the donkey eagerly, and the exchange was made—and that is why snakes renew their youth every year, casting off the old skin and appearing as young and shining as ever.

When Zeus discovered that men could no longer foresee the future, he was rather pleased that the snake had cheated the donkey: for he knew that in the days to come many serpents would bite both men and asses, and that snake-bite produces a worse fever of thirst than anything.

Meanwhile he was busy on a surer punishment for Man: he was making the first woman. Her name was Pandora,* which means 'all-gifted', for all of the Im-

*Pandora (pan-dôr'-ə)

mortals helped to endow her. Clever Hephaestus shaped her out of clay, and lovely Aphrodite gave her beauty, while Hermes taught her cunning and boldness, and Athena dressed her in lovely clothes. Zeus breathed life into her, and then Hermes led her down to earth and brought her to Epimetheus, the thoughtless brother of Prometheus, who lived now more or less as a man among men.

When Epimetheus saw the beauty of Pandora he forgot his brother's warning against accepting any gift from Zeus, and fell in love with her at once.

But meanwhile Pandora brought all the evil upon mankind which Zeus had planned.

In the house of Epimetheus stood a golden box which Prometheus had left there with strict orders that no one was to open it. Epimetheus told his wife this, but she was so curious and inquisitive that life did not seem worth living until she knew what treasure it was that her husband was hiding from her.

So one day when he was out, Pandora crept quietly to the golden casket and lifted the lid. Then with a rush and a cry out came all the ills which beset mankind—diseases, and sorrows, hate, jealousy, lies, theft, cheating, and a hundred others.

Terrified at what she had done, Pandora slammed down the lid. But she raised it again quickly when a little voice cried: 'Let me out too! I am Hope!'

For Prometheus had placed Hope there when he shut up the evil things, so that mankind might not suffer quite so much if Zeus had his way.

TALKING ABOUT THE STORY

1. Prometheus needed help to steal fire and to teach man to use it. What did Prometheus ask Epimetheus to do while he journeyed to the sun? Who else assisted Prometheus? How did each one help?
2. How did the gift of fire change men's lives?
3. The gift of the "fire of the immortals" was more than a gift of light and heat. The fire stolen by Prometheus represented the ability to reason. What is the "light of reason"? What is an "enlightened" person?
4. Was Zeus unfair to Prometheus? Or did Prometheus deserve his punishment? Consider the following:

    Prometheus was quite foresighted. How did his behavior show that he thought ahead? Did he know Zeus would be furious when he gave fire to man? Was Prometheus brave? patient? stubborn? disobedient? Why? What other words would describe him?

    In "The Palace of Olympus" you read that Zeus was "strong, brave, stupid, noisy, violent, conceited." Which of these qualities does he show in this story? Does he show other qualities?
5. What explanations about man and nature are found in this myth?

GREEK WORDS IN OUR LANGUAGE

Thousands of English words are built from Greek roots. You may be familiar with many Greek root words, without realizing it.

1. In "The Story of Prometheus" you read that Pandora means "all-gifted." The Greek root *pan* means "all,"

and *dora* means "gift"; together the two word parts mean "all-gifted." Knowing the meaning of *pan* can help you to figure out the meanings of other words. What does *pandemonium* mean? (How does a *demon* act?) What is a *panorama*? (*Horama* means "view.") What is *pantomime*? (*Mimos* means "mimic.")

2. Prometheus was one of the Titans, the group of giant gods who once ruled the earth. The Titans were incredibly huge and strong. Accordingly, anything of tremendous power, size, or strength may be described as *titanic*. For instance, *titanium* is the name of the strongest metal known. Have you ever faced a *titanic* assignment? Have you ever seen a *titanic* mountain or wave?

IDEAS FOR WRITING

1. If you had been Pandora, would you have opened the box? What if Pandora had left it closed? Would someone else have opened it? Who? When?

2. Suppose Prometheus had taught man how to make rain. How might he have done this? How would man have been affected? Would Zeus have been angry?

3. Why did Zeus want man to live forever? How did Zeus try to make man immortal? Why did his plan fail? What if man had drunk the nectar? What might people be like today?

Write about one of these situations.

Sometimes young gods were bright, quick, and naughty, just as children are today. Hermes, who was especially wily and clever, began his career as God of Thieves on the day he was born.

the trickery of hermes

BY OLIVIA COOLIDGE

Hermes, god of thieves and messenger of Zeus, was full of trickery from the start. His mother, the shy nymph, Maia,* bore him secretly in a deep cave, but since the baby god could walk and talk from his birth, she could not hide him long. In fact, when she laid him in the cradle and turned away to let him sleep, he slipped out behind her back and stole to the cave entrance with mischief in his mind. In the grass outside the gateway he found a great tortoise with a spotted shell and seized on it to play with. He took the shell and from it made a framework, stretching seven strings of sheep-gut upon it. Thus he constructed a new and beautiful instrument, the lyre, a kind of harp, and began to play. It sounded marvelous, and as he plucked the strings, he sang to it stories of his mother and of his father, Zeus, and of

*Maia (mā'-yə)

the cave where he was born and the nymphs that served them there.

Presently, when Hermes tired of his new toy, he laid it in his cradle and slipped forth again to get into some real mischief. Just as the sun was going down, he found a mountain side where a great herd of snow-white cattle grazed, the cattle of the sun. Fifty of these the baby god of thieves separated from the herd and began to drive away, down past the sandy river bed to the hard ground beyond, where it would be more difficult to trace their footprints. To make all safe, with much shouting and running, he turned the cattle and forced them to walk backwards through the sandy place so that Apollo might think they were coming to, not going from, their pasture. To conceal his own footprints from the god, he tied branches, leaves and all, under his feet, making great, shuffling tracks, as though someone had been sweeping the sand with a broom.

In spite of all his cunning he did not get away unseen, for an old man working in a vineyard looked up in wonder as the baby god came past. Hermes had his hands full at the time. He was hurrying to get the cattle away before the sun found out they were gone. Consequently he merely called out to the man and promised him good crops if he would keep silent. Then he raced off after the cattle, letting the old man think what he would.

Hermes drove the herd to a distant meadow by a river and penned them there. He killed two of them in sacrifice to the twelve great gods of Olympus, thinking perhaps that before very long he might be in trouble and need the Olympians' aid. Then he hurried back to his home, stole silently into the hall, and jumped into his cradle. There he covered himself up and tried to look like an innocent little baby, though with the left hand he still kept fingering his lyre beneath the clothes.

When the dawn came, Apollo rose, went to the mountain side as his custom was, and looked down on his cattle. Immediately he noticed the theft and called down to a poor old man who was driving his ox to pasture, asking if he had noticed anything.

"I was working in my vineyard yesterday," said the old man, "when I saw a strange sight. A little child, a baby, with a long staff in his hand was driving away a herd of cattle, running from side to side and forcing them to walk backwards with their heads toward him."

It is hard to conceal things from Apollo because he is the god of prophecy, and immediately he knew about Hermes and who he was, secret as his birth had been. As for tracing the cattle, that was a different matter. The tracks went not only backwards; they went up and down and from side to side, while over all were great sweeping marks. Further along, on the hard ground, there were simply no traces at all. Apollo gave up looking for them. Instead he made off for Maia's cave to confront the baby thief.

Hermes snuggled down inside the bedclothes when he saw Apollo coming, and he hunched himself together as best he could, trying to look very tiny indeed. This was hard for him, since he had grown considerably in his first day. He could not deceive Apollo, who came up to the cradle, demanding angrily, "Where are my cattle, you thief? Tell me at once what you have done with them, or I will cast you down into darkness forever, and you can see how you like thieving there."

Hermes peeped up at him over the edge of the bedclothes and said in a weak little voice, "Why are you shouting at me about cattle? I am just a poor little baby. The only things I care about are good milk and warm baths and soft wrappings. I cannot even walk. As for your cattle, wherever they are, they certainly are not here. I swear it by Zeus, the father of us both."

He looked up at Apollo with such a wide and innocent smile that the god could not help laughing, but he was still angry all the same. He picked up the child from the cradle, coverings and all, and shook him. All he got from that was to find out that Hermes was quick and slippery as an eel and could perfectly well stand on his own feet if he chose. At last Apollo, seeing there was nothing to be done with him, took him by the hand and dragged him off to the throne of Zeus upon Olympus. Here the father of gods had to smile as he saw the two of them, the angry god and the curly-haired, blue-eyed child. Hermes stood before his throne and swore in an innocent, baby voice that the cattle had never come near his house, asking indignantly how an infant could be connected with cattle stealing anyway. Zeus laughed, but he knew perfectly well the truth of the affair, and he bade Hermes go immediately and show Apollo where the cattle lay hid. He meant to have no more nonsense, and Hermes saw that he must be obeyed.

Apollo looked down on the hidden meadow to which the child had led him, and saw his great white cattle contentedly feeding there. Then as his eye fell on the hides of the two slaughtered animals stiffening on a rock, he blazed with anger. "You shall pay for this," he said to Hermes, turning on him threateningly.

This time the boy was really frightened and fell back a foot or two, looking uneasily from one side to the other, but he found no escape. "Wait a moment," he begged hastily. "Wait, listen, I have something for you," and he pulled out his lyre. As the god Apollo heard the wonderful notes and perceived how beautifully they would blend with the voice in song, he was amazed and his anger quite fell from him.

"Where did you get this wonderful thing?" he asked. "Give it me, give it me. Keep my fifty cattle, and I will give you a golden staff in addition for you to herd them with. It seems to me I have to have this and to make music for rich feasts and lovely dances. With this I will comfort sorrow, relive past glories, and melt the heart of stone. I think it will sing of itself for me the moment I touch it, for it knows already that it is mine."

"I will gladly give you the lyre," said the son of Maia, "and take your cattle and your golden wand in return. I will be friends with you as a brother ought to be. From now on I swear that I will never steal anything of yours."

Thus the two became friends, and from that time forward Apollo enchanted the gods of Olympus with the glorious music of his lyre. But Hermes drives the white cattle of the sun across the sky on a windy day, and with his golden rod, around which he has twined two snakes, he charms the eyes of men to sleep and deceives them with dreams and visions. Yet Hermes is good for men also, since he rests and heals them with sleep. Moreover he bears the messages of Zeus, and with these he must often do men service.

WORDS FROM MYTHOLOGY

The Lyre

The lyre is a harplike instrument with two curved arms and four to ten strings. The Greeks used it to accompany singers and poets. *Lyrical* music is very light and melodic. What do you suppose *lyric* poetry is?

The nymphs were lovely nature goddesses, who dwelled in streams, rivers, trees, or mountains. Two of the nymphs were Clytie and Daphne. Each of them reacted to Apollo, the handsome God of the Sun, in a very different way.

BY OLIVIA COOLIDGE

the loves of apollo

Apollo, the young sun god, was more glorious than tongue can describe or than mortal eye can behold. As he drove his golden chariot through the sky he dazzled the whole earth with his splendor. Small wonder, then, that the nymph, Clytie,* fell in love with him. Apollo cared nothing for Clytie and would take no notice of her, so that at last her great longing for him drove her almost to madness. She refused to play with her sister nymphs any more, ate nothing, and drank only dew. All night she stood gazing at the heavens, waiting for her lord to appear. All day she followed him with her eyes as he moved slowly from East to West. At last the gods took pity on her, and since she could not die, they changed her into the tall, thin sunflower, which turns its face towards the sun all day as he moves across the sky.

*Clytie (klī′-ti)

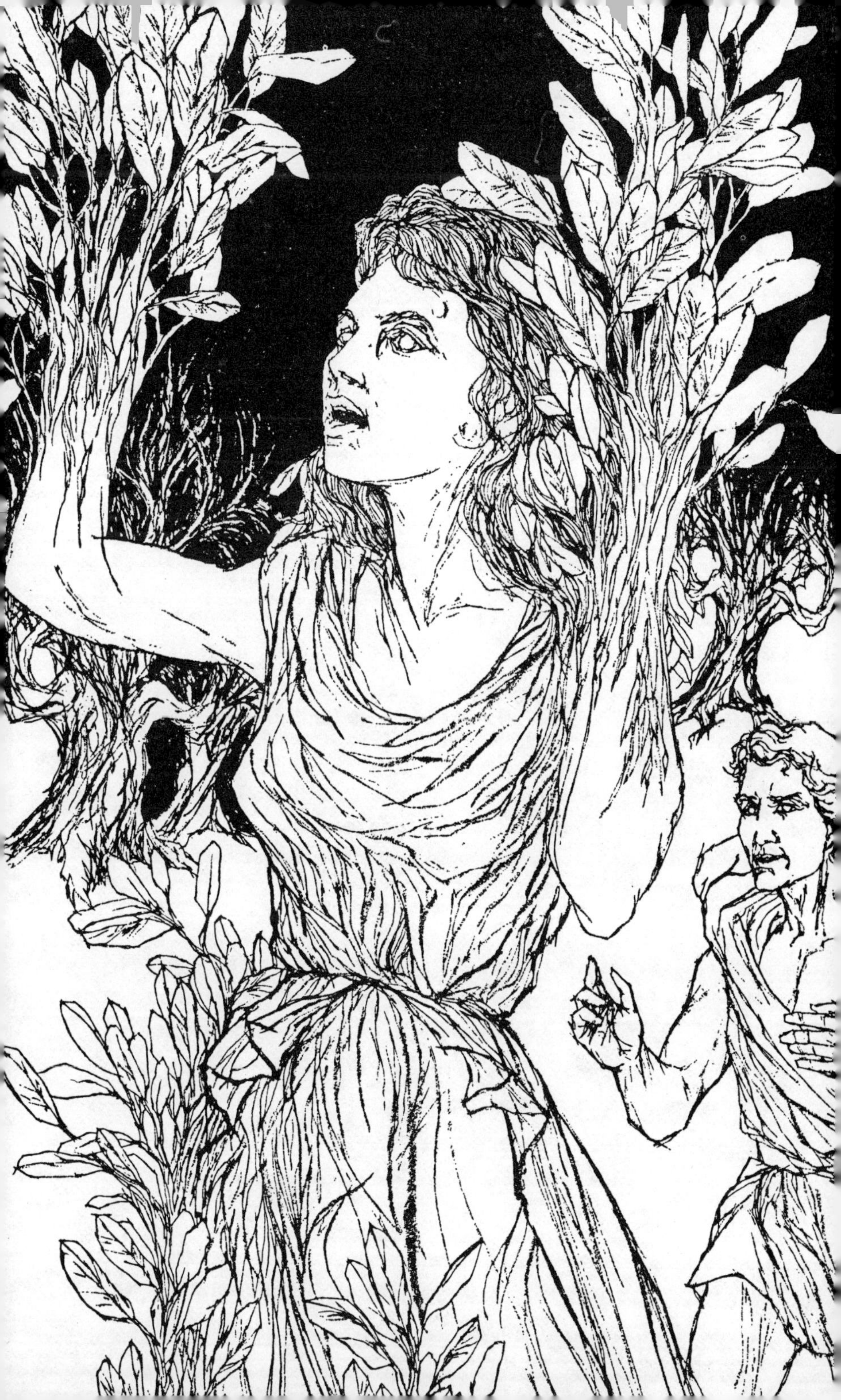

Though Apollo was unkind to Clytie, he too could fall in love. One day in the woods he caught sight of the nymph, Daphne, daughter of a river god. Daphne was fair and white, as river nymphs are, and had rippling dark-green hair. She loved to roam the forests hunting with bow and arrow, and she had vowed to live unmarried like the huntress, Artemis. She, therefore, felt no more love for the god than he had felt for Clytie. Instead she was afraid of him, and when he approached her, she turned and ran from him, her long hair streaming in the wind. More beautiful than ever was she as she ran, and Apollo sped after her, begging her to stop and listen to him, offering her his throne and his palace, telling her not to be afraid. The nearer he came, the more terrified Daphne felt as she raced down the slope towards her father's stream. She felt the radiant warmth of the god behind her, and his hand stretched out to catch her hair. She shrieked to her father to save her, and the river god made answer the only way he could. Suddenly the flight of Daphne was arrested, as her feet took root in the ground. Her body dwindled, her arms shot up, and as Apollo seized her in his arms, he found himself grasping a bush of laurel with shining leaves the color of Daphne's dark-green hair. For a second he felt the frightened heart of the nymph beat beneath the bark enclosing it. Then it was still.

Apollo sorrowed deeply for the loss of his love, and in memory of her he always wore a wreath of laurel. Laurel decorated his lyre, and at his festival the prize for athletes and musicians was a laurel crown.

GREEK CUSTOMS LIVE ON

The Laurel Tree

The laurel tree, an evergreen with shiny stiff leaves, small yellowish flowers, and purple berries, sometimes grows as tall as sixty feet. The Greeks wove small branches and leaves of laurel into wreaths to crown poets, heroes, and athletes. Today winners of the Olympic Games receive laurel wreaths and artists depict poets as if they were crowned with laurel.

If someone received laurels, he would be honored, or crowned with a laurel wreath for a special achievement. Suppose someone told you to "look to your laurels." What would he mean? Suppose someone told you that you could "rest on your laurels." What would this mean?

Even the strong and brave young men of Greek legend were sometimes stubborn and foolhardy. Phaethon was so determined to go on a wild adventure that even his father could not dissuade him.

BY OLIVIA COOLIDGE

phaethon son of apollo

Though Apollo always honored the memory of Daphne, she was not his only love. Another was a mortal, Clymene,* by whom he had a son named Phaethon.* Phaethon grew up with his mother, who, since she was mortal, could not dwell in the halls of Olympus or in the palace of the sun. She lived not far from the East in the land of Ethiopia,* and as her son grew up, she would point to the place where Eos,* goddess of the dawn, lighted up the sky and tell him that there his father dwelt. Phaethon loved to boast of his divine father as he saw the golden chariot riding high through the air. He would remind his comrades of other sons of gods and mortal women who, by virtue of their great deeds, had themselves become gods at last. He must always be first in everything, and in most things this was easy, since he was in truth

*Clymene (klīm'-ə-ni) *Ethiopia (ē'-thi-ō'-pi-ə)
*Phaethon (fā'-ə-t'n) *Eos (ē'-os)

45

stronger, swifter, and more daring than the others. Even if he were not victorious, Phaethon always claimed to be first in honor. He could never bear to be beaten, even if he must risk his life in some rash way to win.

Most of the princes of Ethiopia willingly paid Phaethon honor, since they admired him greatly for his fire and beauty. There was one boy, however, Epaphos,* who was rumored to be a child of Zeus himself. Since this was not certainly proved, Phaethon chose to disbelieve it and to demand from Epaphos the deference that he obtained from all others. Epaphos was proud too, and one day he lost his temper with Phaethon and turned on him, saying, "You are a fool to believe all that your mother tells you. You are all swelled up with false ideas about your father."

Crimson with rage, the lad rushed home to his mother and demanded that she prove to him the truth of the story that she had often told. "Give me some proof," he implored her, "with which I can answer this insult of Epaphos. It is a matter of life and death to me, for if I cannot, I shall die of shame."

"I swear to you," replied his mother solemnly, "by the bright orb of the sun itself that you are his son. If I swear falsely, may I never look on the sun again, but die before the next time he mounts the heavens. More than this I cannot do, but you, my child, can go to the eastern palace of Phoebus Apollo*—it lies not far away—and there speak with the god himself."

The son of Clymene leaped up with joy at his mother's words. The palace of Apollo was indeed not far. It stood just below the eastern horizon, its tall pillars glistening

*Epaphos (ē'-pə-fəs)
*Phoebus Apollo (fē'-bəs ə-pol'-ō)

with bronze and gold. Above these it was white with gleaming ivory, and the great doors were flashing silver, embossed with pictures of earth, sky, and sea, and the gods that dwelt therein. Up the steep hill and the bright steps climbed Phaethon, passing unafraid through the silver doors, and stood in the presence of the sun. Here at last he was forced to turn away his face, for Phoebus sat in state on his golden throne. It gleamed with emeralds and precious stones, while on the head of the god was a brilliant diamond crown upon which no eye could look undazzled.

Phaethon hid his face, but the god had recognized his son, and he spoke kindly, asking him why he had come. Then Phaethon plucked up courage and said, "I come to ask you if you are indeed my father. If you are so, I beg you to give me some proof of it so that men may recognize me as Phoebus' son."

The god smiled, being well pleased with his son's beauty and daring. He took off his crown so that Phaethon could look at him, and coming down from his throne, he put his arms around the boy, and said, "You are indeed my son and Clymene's, and worthy to be called so. Ask of me whatever thing you wish to prove your origin to men, and you shall have it."

Phaethon swayed for a moment and was dizzy with excitement at the touch of the god. His heart leaped; the blood rushed into his face. Now he felt that he was truly divine, unlike other men, and he did not wish to be counted with men any more. He looked up for a moment at his radiant father. "Let me drive the chariot of the sun across the heavens for one day," he said.

Apollo frowned and shook his head. "I cannot break my promise, but I will dissuade you if I can," he answered. "How can you drive my chariot, whose horses need a strong hand on the reins? The climb is too steep for you. The immense height will make you dizzy. The swift streams of air in the upper heaven will sweep you off your course. Even the immortal gods could not drive my chariot. How then can you? Be wise and make some other choice."

The pride of Phaethon was stubborn, for he thought the god was merely trying to frighten him. Besides, if he could guide the sun's chariot, would he not have proved his right to be divine rather than mortal? For that he would risk his life. Indeed, once he had seen Apollo's splendor, he did not wish to go back and live among men. Therefore, he insisted on his right until Apollo had to give way.

When the father saw that nothing else would satisfy the boy, he bade the Hours bring forth his chariot and yoke the horses. The chariot was of gold and had two gold-rimmed wheels with spokes of silver. In it there was room for one man to stand and hold the reins. Around the front and sides of it ran a rail, but the back was open. At the end of a long pole there were yokes for the four horses. The pole was of gold and shone with precious jewels: the golden topaz, the bright diamond, the green emerald, and the flashing ruby. While the Hours were yoking the swift, pawing horses, rosy-fingered Dawn hastened to the gates of heaven to draw them open. Meanwhile Apollo anointed his son's face with a magic ointment, that he might be able to bear the heat

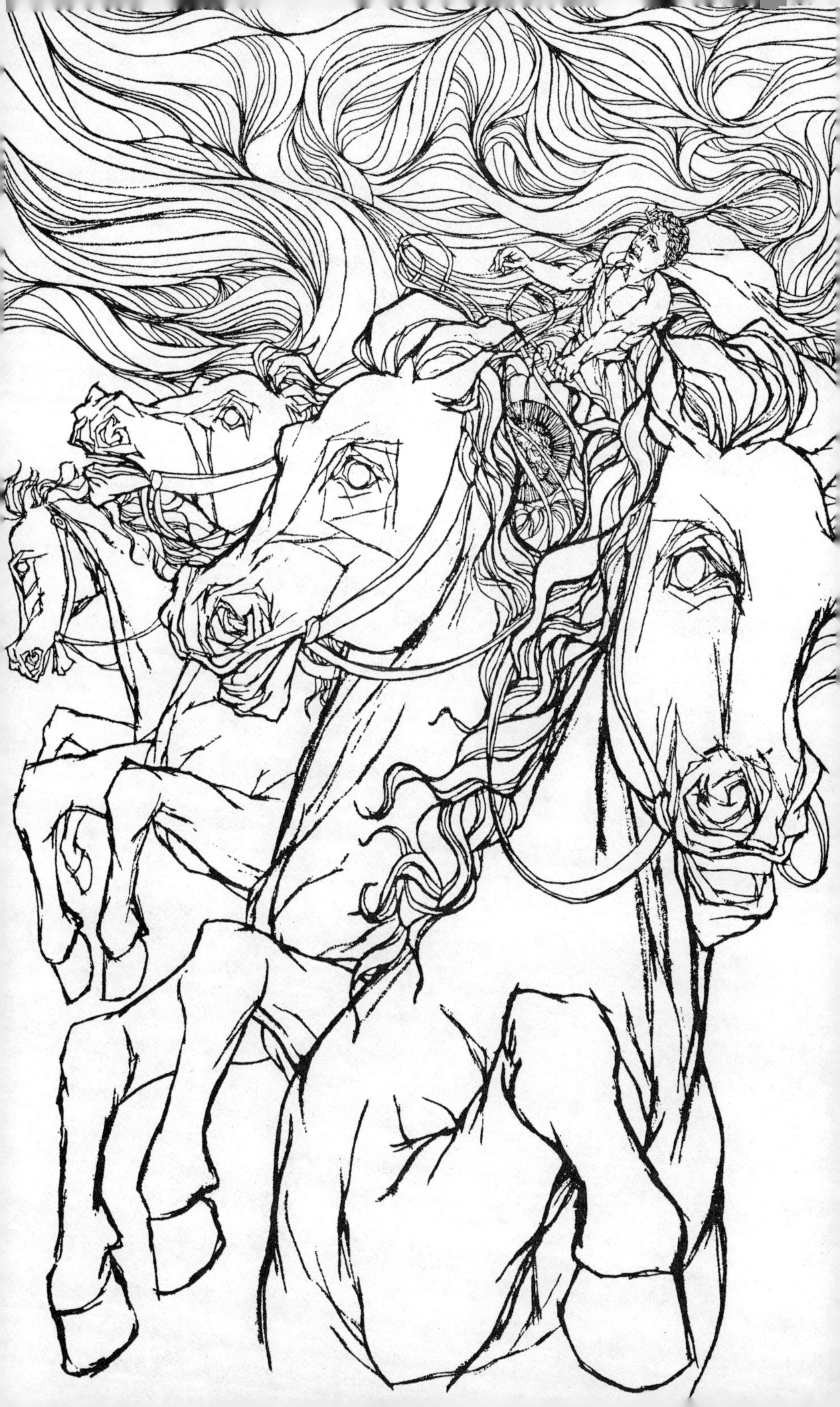

of the fire-breathing horses and the golden chariot. At last Phaethon mounted the chariot and grasped the reins, the barriers were let down, and the horses shot up into the air.

At first the fiery horses sped forward up the accustomed trail, but behind them the chariot was too light without the weight of the immortal god. It bounded from side to side and was dashed up and down. Phaethon was too frightened and too dizzy to pull the reins, nor would he have known anyway whether he was on the usual path. As soon as the horses felt that there was no hand controlling them, they soared up, up with fiery speed into the heavens till the earth grew pale and cold beneath them. Phaethon shut his eyes, trembling at the dizzy, precipitous height. Then the horses dropped down, more swiftly than a falling stone, flinging themselves madly from side to side in panic because they were masterless. Phaethon dropped the reins entirely and clung with all his might to the chariot rail. Meanwhile as they came near the earth, it dried up and cracked apart. Meadows were reduced to white ashes, cornfields smoked and shriveled, cities perished in flame. Far and wide on the wooded mountains the forests were ablaze, and even the snow-clad Alps were bare and dry. Rivers steamed and dried to dust. The great North African plain was scorched until it became the desert that it is today. Even the sea shrank back to pools and caves, until dried fishes were left baking upon the white-hot sands. At last the great earth mother called upon Zeus to save her from utter destruction, and Zeus hurled a mighty thunderbolt at the unhappy Phaethon, who was still crouched in the chariot, clinging desperately to the rail. The dart cast him out, and he fell flaming in a long trail through the air. The chariot broke in pieces at the mighty blow, and the maddened horses rushed snorting back to the stable of their master, Apollo.

Unhappy Clymene and her daughters wandered over the whole earth seeking the body of the boy they loved so well. When they found him, they took him and buried him. Over his grave they wept and could not be comforted. At last the gods in pity for their grief changed them into poplar trees, which weep with tears of amber in memory of Phaethon.

TALKING ABOUT THE STORIES

1. Characters in the stories you have just read had faults that caused their own downfalls. Can you remember:

    Who got into trouble because he was stubborn? How did his obstinacy cause trouble?

    Who got into trouble because of his mischievous spirit? Why did this happen?

    Who caused his own disappointment by being too eager? How did he do this?

2. Did any of the characters in these stories remind you of people you know? How? Were their personalities made up of good traits, bad traits, or combinations of both?

3. In "The Story of Prometheus" Zeus was a wrathful god. Did the stormy side of his nature show in "The Trickery of Hermes"? How would you describe his disposition when he mediated between Apollo and Hermes?

What personality traits did Apollo show in these stories? How did he respond to Hermes's pranks? How did Apollo behave in other instances?

EXPRESSIONS FROM MYTHOLOGY

Have you ever heard people describe something by making a comparison? Maybe you've read or used expressions like these: a mountain "as high as Olympus"; a cliff "as jagged as lightning"; applause "as loud as thunder."

Can you think of other expressions that make comparisons? What effect do these expressions have on conversation and writing?

Try creating your own expressions using qualities of gods, goddesses, or other characters. You might already have a few in mind: "as stubborn as Phaethon"; "as jealous as Hera."

IDEAS FOR WRITING

Write a story about a person who has a flaw that causes trouble. You may want to include the person's good qualities, too.

Hera became very suspicious whenever Zeus left Mount Olympus to visit the earth. She followed after him, attempting to watch him and control his actions. Sometimes, while trying to outsmart Zeus, Hera interfered with the lives of nymphs and mortals.

Echo and Narcissus

BY KATHARINE PYLE

At times it pleased great Zeus to take upon himself some earthly form, and so descend from Olympus, and amuse himself among the mortals for a time.

But Hera, his queen, was jealous of these pleasures, and whenever she learned that he had gone, she would follow him and search the whole world through until she found him. Then she would weary him with angry words and with reproaches till, for the sake of peace, he would return with her to his high palace on Olympus.

But once, when Hera followed him there he hid himself in a deep wood, and bade the nymph Echo go to meet his queen and keep her for a while in talk until he could escape unseen back to Olympus.

This Echo did. Of all the nymphs she was the wittiest and the most cunning. She hastened forth, and meeting the goddess on her way began at once to pour into her ears some curious tale of something she had lately seen. So strange was the tale that, though Hera was in haste, she stayed to listen. Then when the story had reached its end, she would have gone again upon her way, but now it was some even stranger tale Echo had to tell. So she kept Hera listening there till Zeus was safely back upon Olympus. His queen found him there when she returned at last, outwearied from her searching on the earth. He was enthroned again in his high hall in all his majesty and glory.

But Hera guessed the trick that had been played upon her, and in wrath she cried, "Never again shall Echo's cunning tongue be used for deceiving others. All her wit shall now avail her nothing, for she shall never again be able to put into words her cunning thoughts," and she took from Echo all power of speech, except that of repeating what she heard others say.

Now piteous indeed was Echo's case, and the more piteous because she loved a youth named Narcissus.* He was the fairest youth on all the earth; so beauteous, indeed, that many a nymph had pined for love of him, but Narcissus scorned them all and fled from their sighs and tender looks. Echo might, perhaps, in time have won his love by her wit, if she could have put it into words, but now she could not, and he fled from her as from the others.

But one day she hid herself among the bushes in a wood where he often came, with the hope that, thinking himself alone, he might breathe out some tender word or sigh she could repeat to him.

*Narcissus (när-sis'-əs)

It was not long before she saw him come. He was weary from the chase, and threw himself down beneath a tree to rest. "Heigho!" he sighed.

"Heigho!" Echo repeated softly.

"Who is there?" cried Narcissus, starting up.

"Is there!" answered Echo.

"Is it a friend?"

"A friend!" replied the nymph.

"Then come to me."

"Come to me," Echo cried joyously, and springing from the thicket where she had lain hidden, she ran to him with outstretched arms.

But Narcissus drew back from her with frowning brows. "I know thee now," he cried. "Thou art one of those who have followed me. I do not want thy love."

"Want thy love," the nymph repeated piteously, holding out to him her arms.

But Narcissus answered more sharply still, "Away and touch me not and never follow me again!"

"Follow me again!" cried Echo. But already Narcissus was gone from her. He had fled away more swiftly than she could follow him, and from that day he hid from her so that she could not find him.

Then the poor nymph grieved bitterly. Day after day she spent in tears and sad complaints until at last her sorrow melted her flesh away; her bones became rocks, and at last nothing was left of her but a wandering voice that haunted caves and cliffs, answering back the calls and cries of others. But before she had vanished quite, the nymph breathed out a silent prayer to Aphrodite that some day Narcissus himself might feel a sorrow like to hers, might pine with love of one who neither could nor would return that love.

Her silent prayer was granted, and thus it came to pass that Narcissus entered once a lonely wood where he had never been before, and there came to a pool as still and bright as polished silver. Never deer or bird or any living thing had found that pool until Narcissus came. Thirsty after his wanderings he knelt to drink, and as he bent above the pool he saw himself reflected in the water, yet he did not know it was his own image that he saw. He thought it was some nymph or naiad who lived there in the pool—one lovelier far than any he had ever seen before.

Filled with delight he gazed, then suddenly plunged his arms down in the pool and sought to seize the lovely thing, but at once the water broke into ripples and his reflection disappeared.

Narcissus drew back with beating heart, and breathlessly waited hoping it would again appear, yet fearing that he had frightened it away forever.

Then, as the pool grew still, his image showed again there in the water. More gently now Narcissus moved, stooping down toward it, and always as he stooped near and nearer, so the image seemed to rise up toward him, until it was as though in a moment their lips would meet; but when he thought to kiss those lips, 'twas only the chill water that he touched.

Again and still again he tried to grasp the image, but always at his touch it disappeared. And now the unhappy youth spent all his days there by the pool, filled with hopeless love of his own image. He neither ate nor slept, but pined and pined with love, even as Echo had, until at last he pined his life away.

Then from the fields and woods arose a sound of mourning. Voices cried, "Narcissus, the beautiful, is dead! is dead!" Youths and nymphs, dryads and fauns, lamented over him, while Echo repeated every sigh and sad complaint she heard.

A funeral pyre was built on which they thought to lay the lovely form of dead Narcissus, but when they went to look for it, it had disappeared; instead they found only, in the spot where it had lain, a snow-white flower; it was a flower different from any they had ever seen before, and guessing that the gods had changed him into this form, they called it by his name, and ever since that flower has been known everywhere as the Narcissus—loveliest of blooms, even as of old that first Narcissus was the loveliest of youths.

WORDS FROM MYTHOLOGY

Echo

> The story of Echo provides one explanation for the *echoes* in canyons and cavernous rooms. How? What is the scientific explanation of an *echo*?

Narcissist

> A *narcissist* is an individual who has become so egotistical and concerned for himself that he has no thoughts or feelings for anyone else. Why are such individuals named after Narcissus?

One day Athena, Goddess of Wisdom and Handicrafts, flew into a rage because a maiden dared to offend her. Arachne should have remembered that the gods usually punished mortals who displeased them.

arachne

BY KATHARINE PYLE

There was once a girl named **Arachne,*** who could spin and weave so skillfully that it was said no one in all the world could equal her. This she herself believed, and she became so proud and vain she thought herself better than any others. She even scorned her parents, who were humble folk.

Her father dyed the wool and flax she used, and this he did so skillfully that Arachne had her choice of almost every shade and tint from Tyrian* purple, crimson, and deep blue to palest shades of amber, rose, and green; these she wove into patterns new and strange, each different and each, so it would seem, more beautiful than the others.

People came from far and near to see her work, and even the nymphs left their fields and woods to gather round her loom and watch her weaving.

Once, as they watched her thus, she heard them whispering among themselves, "Surely

*Arachne (ə-rak′-ni)
*Tyrian (tir′-i-ən)

59

Athena herself must have taught Arachne how to weave; how else could a mortal maiden have such skill."

But this offended Arachne, and she cried out angrily, "Athena hath taught me nothing. All that I know I learned of myself, and I will dare to say that if Athena in person were to come and try her skill with mine, she scarcely could outdo me. Nay, I will say more than that; I doubt if she could even equal me."

These boasting words frightened the nymphs, so that they fled away to the woods and hid themselves. They feared Athena's wrath might fall not only on the maid who boasted thus, but even upon those who listened to her.

The goddess indeed, had long since noticed the pride and vanity of Arachne, and now she decided to teach the girl a lesson; so she took on herself the form of an old woman, wrinkled and bent, and meanly clad, and in this form she appeared before Arachne, and spoke to her. "Proud girl," she said, "thy boasts are like thyself, both vain and foolish. How dost thou dare to think that any mortal maid could equal a goddess in her skill? Dost thou not fear thy pride may bring down on thy head the wrath of Athena?"

Arachne, at these words from one who seemed so old and poor, was filled with anger, and she cried, "If what I said were only vain boasting, then let Athena come and prove it. I am ready here and now to try my skill with hers. If I fail, I will most willingly accept whatever punishment she may choose to lay upon me, but if I win, then let her own before both gods and men that my skill is greater than her own. Only let her come."

"She is already here," Athena answered, and with these words her disguise dropped from her, and she stood forth before Arachne in all her brightness and her majesty. Then the girl trembled, but Athena cried, "Come, now, set up thy loom, and I will set up mine beside it, and we will try our skill against each other as thou hast said."

Arachne was still somewhat afraid, but presently she gathered her courage together, and set up her loom; Athena's was put close beside it, and the two took their places. With skillful hands they stretched their woofs, smoothly and tightly across either loom, and then took up their shuttles, and began to weave. Their hands flew so swiftly back and forth that the eye could not follow them. Soon colors and designs began to show upon the looms.

On Athena's web was pictured forth the glories of the gods, the mighty deeds of heroes, and the rewards that had been meted out to them. There Zeus was shown reigning high above the heavens, with many of the gods and goddesses gathered about him; there was shown Phoebus* driving his shining chariot across the sky, and shedding down light and happiness on mankind; Ceres* in bounteous kindness led out the harvesters to the fields of ripened grain; the hero Perseus* was shown slaying the monster Medusa;* Bellerophon* soaring on the winged horse Pegasus* to slay the flaming dragon Chimera;* Aphrodite mourning in tender grief over Adonis; Princess Andromeda* lifted up to heaven and throned among the stars. All these and many other things Athena pictured forth with immortal skill and beauty. Last of all

*Phoebus (fē'-bəs)
*Ceres (sêr'-ēz)
*Perseus (pūr'-sūs)
*Medusa (mə-doo'-sə)
*Bellerophon (bə-ler'-ə-fon')
*Pegasus (peg'-ə-səs)
*Chimera (kə-mēr'-ə)
*Andromeda (an-drom'-i-də)

she wove about the whole a border of the pale olive blooms and fruit beloved of gods. So was her task complete.

But Arachne's web was of a different kind. She chose to picture with her threads all the evil deeds the gods had done. There was shown the earth torn and destroyed while Titans and the gods battled together. There was shown Prometheus bound in misery, while vultures tore at him; Atlas wearily bearing up the weight of all the heavens; Europa, the princess who was carried off by Zeus in the form of a bull; Niobe,* the queen who asked to be worshipped as a goddess, weeping over her children slain as punishment by the gods; there were shown wretched mortals being turned by jealous goddesses to beasts or serpents or to stones; pictures of these and many other evil things Arachne wove upon her loom, and all with such skill that every god and goddess might be known and told from each other. Then last she wove about it all a border of such flowers as Persephone,* Ceres' daughter, had dropped when Hades stole her from the bright upper world and carried her down to the dark realm of spirits.

So her task, too, was finished.

But when Athena looked and saw what she had done, she was filled with rage. She struck the shuttle from Arachne's hand, and tearing the web from the loom, she rent it up and down and trampled it underfoot.

"Thou wretched one!" she cried. "Hast thou no reverence? Dost thou even dare to mock the gods themselves? But thou shalt not go unpunished. Never again

*Niobe (ni'-ə-bi)
*Persephone (pĕr-sef'-ə-ni)

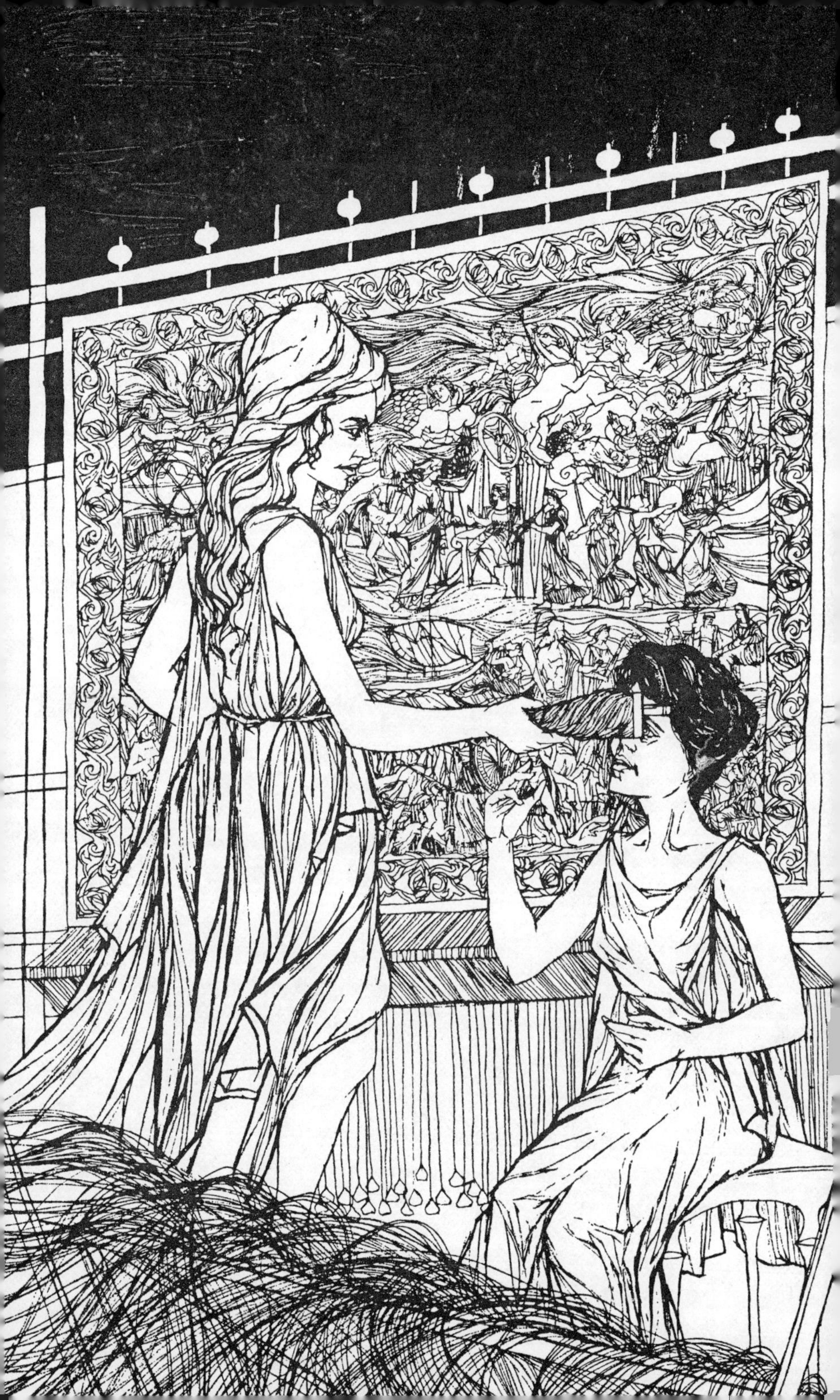

shall thy too skillful hands drive the shuttle back and forth, to picture out thy evil and irreverent thoughts!"

So saying, she struck Arachne on her forehead with her shuttle. At once all power left Arachne's hands and arms. She could not lift them up, she could not move her fingers even, though she strove with all her might. Then in despair, she cried, "Take not away my power of weaving, O Athena! rather take my life; better to die than live helpless and scorned by all."

Then Athena, even in her anger, pitied her, and said, "Thou shalt keep thy life, and even keep thy power to weave; but not as before."

Again she touched Arachne's forehead with her shuttle, but gently now.

Then a strange thing was seen, for Arachne, at that touch, began to change and shrink. Smaller and smaller still she grew. Her body became round, her color grey, her head so small it scarcely could be seen, her soft arms disappeared, and on each side she had instead three thin, long, agile legs. By Athena's will she had been changed into an insect, one different from any other insect in the world, the first of all the spiders. She was a spinner still; Athena had left with her her power to weave as she had promised, but she now could show no colors and no pictures on her webs. The power of making such was gone from her. They all were alike, all thin and white and frail, so that the merest, lightest touch could break the threads, and tear them into shreds.

Arachne in time had children; they were spiders, too, and they had children of their own, until at last there were thousands of spiders in the world, all spinning webs; but all those webs were plain and colorless and frail as were the ones that their first mother wove after she lost her human form, and by Athena's will was humbled and brought low.

WORDS FROM MYTHOLOGY

Arachnid

>*Arachnida* is the scientific name for a group of animals. Can you guess what *arachnids* are?

Athenaeum

>A library or a scientific association is sometimes called an *athenaeum*. The *Athenaeum* was a Greek school established for the study of the arts. After what goddess was this institution named? Why?

Sometimes the Greek gods and goddesses punished people by changing them into plants or animals. At other times, they rewarded mortals that way.

BY EDITH HAMILTON

ceyx and alcyone

Ceyx,* a king in Thessaly,* was the son of Lucifer, the light-bearer, the star that brings in the day, and all his father's bright gladness was in his face. His wife Alcyone* was also of high descent; she was the daughter of Aeolus,* King of the Winds. The two loved each other devotedly and were never willingly apart. Nevertheless, a time came when he decided he must leave her and make a long journey across the sea. Various matters had happened to disturb him and he wished to consult the oracle, men's refuge in trouble. When Alcyone learned what he was planning she was overwhelmed with grief and terror. She told him with streaming tears and in a voice broken with sobs, that she knew as few others could the power of the winds upon the sea. In her father's palace she had watched them from her childhood, their stormy meetings, the black clouds they summoned and the wild red light-

*Ceyx (sē'-iks)
*Thessaly (thes'-ə-li)
*Alcyone (al-sī'-ə-ni)
*Aeolus (ē'-ə-ləs)

67

ning. "And many a time upon the beach," she said, "I have seen the broken planks of ships tossed up. Oh, do not go. But if I cannot persuade you, at least take me with you. I can endure whatever comes to us together."

Ceyx was deeply moved, for she loved him no better than he loved her, but his purpose held fast. He felt that he must get counsel from the oracle and he would not hear of her sharing the perils of the voyage. She had to yield and let him go alone. Her heart was so heavy when she bade him farewell it was as if she foresaw what was to come. She waited on the shore watching the ship until it sailed out of sight.

That very night a fierce storm broke over the sea. The winds all met in a mad hurricane, and the waves rose up mountain-high. Rain fell in such sheets that the whole heaven seemed falling into the sea and the sea seemed leaping up into the sky. The men on the quivering, battered boat were mad with terror, all except one who thought only of Alcyone and rejoiced that she was in safety. Her name was on his lips when the ship sank and the waters closed over him.

Alcyone was counting off the days. She kept herself busy, weaving a robe for him against his return and another for herself to be lovely in when he first saw her. And many times each day she prayed to the gods for him, to Juno most of all. The goddess was touched by those prayers for one who had long been dead. She summoned her messenger Iris and ordered her to go to the house of Somnus,* God of Sleep, and bid him send a dream to Alcyone to tell her the truth about Ceyx.

The abode of Sleep is near the black country of the Cimmerians, in a deep valley where the sun never shines

*Somnus (som'-nəs)

and dusky twilight wraps all things in shadows. No cock crows there; no watchdog breaks the silence; no branches rustle in the breeze; no clamor of tongues disturbs the peace. The only sound comes from the gently flowing stream of Lethe,* the river of forgetfulness, where the waters murmuring entice to sleep. Before the door poppies bloom, and other drowsy herbs. Within, the God of Slumber lies upon a couch downy-soft and black of hue. There came Iris in her cloak of many colors, trailing across the sky in a rainbow curve, and the dark house was lit up with the shining of her garments. Even so, it was hard for her to make the god open his heavy eyes and understand what he was required to do. As soon as she was sure he was really awake and her errand done, Iris sped away, fearful that she too might sink forever into slumber.

The old God of Sleep aroused his son, Morpheus,* skilled in assuming the form of any and every human being, and he gave him Juno's orders. On noiseless wings Morpheus flew through the darkness and stood by Alcyone's bed. He had taken on the face and form of Ceyx drowned. Naked and dripping wet he bent over her couch. "Poor wife," he said, "look, your husband is here. Do you know me or is my face changed in death? I am dead, Alcyone. Your name was on my lips when the waters overwhelmed me. There is no hope for me any more. But give me your tears. Let me not go down to the shadowy land unwept." In her sleep Alcyone moaned and stretched her arms out to clasp him. She cried aloud, "Wait for me. I will go with you," and her cry awakened her. She woke to the conviction that her husband was dead, that what she had seen was no dream, but him-

*Lethe (lē'-thi)   *Morpheus (môr'-fi-əs)

self. "I saw him, on that very spot," she told herself. "So piteous he looked. He is dead and soon I shall die. Could I stay here when his dear body is tossed about in the waves? I will not leave you, my husband; I will not try to live."

With the first daylight she went to the shore, to the headland where she had stood to watch him sail away. As she gazed seaward, far off on the water she saw something floating. The tide was setting in and the thing came nearer and nearer until she knew it was a dead body. She watched it with pity and horror in her heart as it drifted slowly toward her. And now it was close to the headland, almost beside her. It was he, Ceyx, her husband. She ran and leaped into the water, crying, "Husband, dearest!"—and then oh, wonder, instead of sinking into the waves she was flying over them. She had wings; her body was covered with feathers. She had been changed into a bird. The gods were kind. They did the same to Ceyx. As she flew to the body it was gone, and he, changed into a bird like herself, joined her. But their love was unchanged. They are always seen together, flying or riding the waves.

Every year there are seven days on end when the sea lies still and calm; no breath of wind stirs the waters. These are the days when Alcyone broods over her nest floating on the sea. After the young birds are hatched the charm is broken; but each winter these days of perfect peace come, and they are called after her, Alcyone, or, more commonly, Halcyon days,

> While birds of calm sit brooding on the charmèd wave.

TALKING ABOUT THE STORIES

1. The Greeks believed that mortals who displeased the gods almost always received punishment from Olympus. Tell how each of the following characters offended a god: Echo, Narcissus, Arachne. How was each one punished?

    People in many early societies believed that a punishment should suit a crime. This was called "eye for eye, tooth for tooth" punishment. For instance, if a man burned someone else's hut, his tribe might torture him with fire. Do you think the Greeks believed in this form of justice? Why?

2. Sometimes the gods took pity on sufferers and tried to give them a measure of relief. Whom did the gods pity? How did they show it? Can you remember examples of the gods' mercy from other stories in this book?

WORDS FROM MYTHOLOGY

1. When problems arose, the Greeks sometimes consulted priests and priestesses called oracles. The oracles sat on three-legged stools to communicate with the gods, and often made their revelations in words that were very puzzling. These revelations gave a warning, advised a certain action, or predicted the future. They often required interpretation.

2. Do the italicized words in the following sentences remind you of the names of characters in "Ceyx and Alcyone"?

> Doctors sometimes use the drug *morphine* to relieve the pain and suffering of patients.
>
> A sleepwalker is called a *somnambulist*.
>
> The Latin god Somnus is called Hypnos in Greek. *Hypnotism* can induce a state like *somnambulism*.

What is the meaning of each italicized word? How is it related to the god on whose name the word is based?

IDEAS FOR WRITING

1. Suppose that you have displeased a god and that he plans to punish you by turning you into a plant or an animal. You want him to give you a choice of the plant or animal you will become. Write about what you did to make the god angry and about the arguments you would use to get your way.

2. You have now read at least fifteen explanations the Greeks made up to explain their surroundings. How many of these explanations can you recall?

   Pretend that you, like the ancient Greeks, have no knowledge of science. You are puzzled by nature. Why do cats have whiskers? Why can the cockroach run so fast? Why does the hyena laugh? Why is the cranberry red? Where does snow come from? Write an original myth explaining the answer to one of these questions or to a different question that you prefer.

Ceres, the Roman goddess of agriculture, oversaw the planting and harvesting of crops. Pluto, king of the underworld, ruled the land of the dead.

One year Ceres and Pluto were in competition with each other. This is the story of their rivalry.

the pomegranate seeds

BY NATHANIEL HAWTHORNE

Mother Ceres* was exceedingly fond of her daughter Proserpina,* and seldom let her go alone into the fields. But, just at the time when my story begins, the good lady was very busy, because she had the care of the wheat, and the Indian corn, and the rye and barley, and, in short, of the crops of every kind, all over the earth; and as the season had thus far been uncommonly backward, it was necessary to make the harvest ripen more speedily than usual. So she put on her turban, made of poppies (a kind of flower which she was always noted for wearing), and got into her car drawn by a pair of winged dragons, and was just ready to set off.

"Dear mother," said Proserpina, "I shall be very lonely while you are away. May I not run

*Ceres (sēr'-ēz)
*Proserpina (prō-sūr'-pi-nə)

down to the shore, and ask some of the sea-nymphs to come up out of the waves and play with me?"

"Yes, child," answered Mother Ceres. "The sea-nymphs are good creatures, and will never lead you into any harm. But you must take care not to stray away from them, nor go wandering about the fields by yourself. Young girls, without their mothers to take care of them, are very apt to get into mischief."

The child promised to be as prudent as if she were a grown-up woman, and, by the time the winged dragons had whirled the car out of sight, she was already on the shore, calling to the sea-nymphs to come and play with her. They knew Proserpina's voice, and were not long in showing their glistening faces and sea-green hair above the water, at the bottom of which was their home. They brought along with them a great many beautiful shells, and, sitting down on the moist sand, where the surf wave broke over them, they busied themselves in making a necklace, which they hung round Proserpina's neck. By way of showing her gratitude, the child besought them to go with her a little way into the fields, so that they might gather abundance of flowers, with which she would make each of her kind playmates a wreath.

"Oh no, dear Proserpina," cried the sea-nymphs; "we dare not go with you upon the dry land. We are apt to grow faint, unless at every breath we can snuff up the salt breeze of the ocean. And don't you see how careful we are to let the surf wave break over us every moment or two, so as to keep ourselves comfortably moist? If it were not for that, we should soon look like bunches of uprooted sea-weed dried in the sun."

"It is a great pity," said Proserpina. "But do you wait for me here, and I will run and gather my apron full of flowers, and be back again before the surf wave has broken ten times over you. I long to make you some wreaths that shall be as lovely as this necklace of many-colored shells."

"We will wait, then," answered the sea-nymphs. "But while you are gone, we may as well lie down on a bank of soft sponge, under the water. The air today is a little too dry for our comfort. But we will pop up our heads every few minutes to see if you are coming."

The young Proserpina ran quickly to a spot where, only the day before, she had seen a great many flowers. These, however, were now a little past their bloom; and wishing to give her friends the freshest and loveliest blossoms, she strayed farther into the fields, and found some that made her scream with delight. Never had she met with such exquisite flowers before,—violets, so large and fragrant,—roses, with so rich and delicate a blush,—such superb hyacinths and such aromatic pinks,—and many others, some of which seemed to be of new shapes and colors. Two or three times, moreover, she could not help thinking that a tuft of most splendid flowers had suddenly sprouted out of the earth before her very eyes, as if on purpose to tempt her a few steps farther. Proserpina's apron was soon filled and brimming over with delightful blossoms. She was on the point of turning back in order to rejoin the sea-nymphs, and sit with them on the moist sands, all twining wreaths together. But, a little farther on, what should she behold? It was a large shrub, completely covered with the most magnificent flowers in the world.

"The darlings!" cried Proserpina; and then she thought to herself, "I was looking at that spot only a moment ago. How strange it is that I did not see the flowers!"

The nearer she approached the shrub, the more attractive it looked, until she came quite close to it; and then, although its beauty was richer than words can tell, she hardly knew whether to like it or not. It bore above a hundred flowers of the most brilliant hues, and each different from the others, but all having a kind of resemblance among themselves, which showed them to be sister blossoms. But there was a deep, glossy lustre on the leaves of the shrub, and on the petals of the flowers, that made Proserpina doubt whether they might not be poisonous. To tell you the truth, as foolish as it may seem, she was half inclined to turn round and run away.

"What a silly child I am!" thought she, taking courage. "It is really the most beautiful shrub that ever sprang out of the earth. I will pull it up by the roots, and carry it home, and plant it in my mother's garden."

Holding up her apron full of flowers with her left hand, Proserpina seized the large shrub with the other, and pulled and pulled, but was hardly able to loosen the soil about its roots. What a deep-rooted plant it was! Again the girl pulled with all her might, and observed that the earth began to stir and crack to some distance around the stem. She gave another pull, but relaxed her hold, fancying that there was a rumbling sound right beneath her feet. Did the roots extend down into some enchanted cavern? Then, laughing at herself for so childish a notion, she made another effort; up came the shrub, and Proserpina staggered back, holding the stem triumphantly in her hand, and gazing at the deep hole which its roots had left in the soil.

Much to her astonishment, this hole kept spreading wider and wider, and growing deeper and deeper, until it really seemed to have no bottom; and all the while, there came a rumbling noise out of its depths, louder and louder, and nearer and nearer, and sounding like the tramp of horses' hoofs and the rattling of wheels. Too much frightened to run away, she stood straining her eyes into this wonderful cavity, and soon saw a team of four sable horses, snorting smoke out of their nostrils, and tearing their way out of the earth with a splendid golden chariot whirling at their heels. There they were, tossing their black manes, flourishing their black tails, and curvetting with every one of their hoofs off the ground at once, close by the spot where Proserpina stood. In the chariot sat the figure of a man, richly dressed, with a crown on his head, all flaming with diamonds. He was of a noble aspect, and rather handsome, but looked sullen and discontented; and he kept rubbing his eyes and shading them with his hand, as if he did not live enough in the sunshine to be very fond of its light.

As soon as this personage saw the affrighted Proserpina, he beckoned her to come a little nearer.

"Do not be afraid," said he, with as cheerful a smile as he knew how to put on. "Come! Will not you like to ride a little way with me, in my beautiful chariot?"

But Proserpina was so alarmed, that she wished for nothing but to get out of his reach. And no wonder. The stranger did not look remarkably good-natured, in spite of his smile; and as for his voice, its tones were deep and stern, and sounded as much like the rumbling of an earthquake under ground as anything else. As is always the case with children in trouble, Proserpina's first thought was to call for her mother.

"Mother, Mother Ceres!" cried she, all in a tremble. "Come quickly and save me."

But her voice was too faint for her mother to hear. Indeed, it is most probable that Ceres was then a thousand miles off, making the corn grow in some far-distant country. Nor could it have availed her poor daughter, even had she been within hearing; for no sooner did Proserpina begin to cry out, than the stranger leaped to the ground, caught the child in his arms, and again mounting the chariot, shook the reins, and shouted to the four black horses to set off. They immediately broke into so swift a gallop that it seemed rather like flying through the air than running along the earth. In a moment, Proserpina lost sight of the pleasant vale of Enna, in which she had always dwelt. Another instant, and even the summit of Mount Ætna* had become so blue in the distance, that she could scarcely distinguish it from the smoke that gushed out of its crater. But still the poor child screamed, and scattered her apron full of flowers along the way, and left a long cry trailing behind the chariot; and many mothers, to whose ears it came, ran quickly to see if any mischief had befallen their children. But Mother Ceres was a great way off, and could not hear the cry.

As they rode on, the stranger did his best to soothe her.

*Aetna (et'-nə)

"Why should you be so frightened, my pretty child?" said he, trying to soften his rough voice. "I promise not to do you any harm. What! You have been gathering flowers? Wait till we come to my palace, and I will give you a garden full of prettier flowers than those, all made of pearls, and diamonds, and rubies. Can you guess who I am? They call my name Pluto, and I am the king of diamonds and all other precious stones. Every atom of the gold and silver that lies under the earth belongs to me, to say nothing of the copper and iron, and of the coal-mines, which supply me with abundance of fuel. Do you see this splendid crown upon my head? You may have it for a plaything. Oh, we shall be very good friends, and you will find me more agreeable than you expect, when once we get out of this troublesome sunshine."

"Let me go home!" cried Proserpina,—"let me go home!"

"My home is better than your mother's," answered King Pluto. "It is a palace, all made of gold, with crystal windows; and because there is little or no sunshine thereabouts, the apartments are illuminated with diamond lamps. You never saw anything half so magnificent as my throne. If you like, you may sit down on it, and be my little queen, and I will sit on the footstool."

"I don't care for golden palaces and thrones," sobbed Proserpina. "Oh, my mother, my mother! Carry me back to my mother!"

But King Pluto, as he called himself, only shouted to his steeds to go faster.

"Pray do not be foolish, Proserpina," said he, in rather a sullen tone. "I offer you my palace and my crown, and all the riches that are under the earth; and you treat me as if I were doing you an injury. The one thing which my palace needs is a merry little maid to run up stairs and down, and cheer up the rooms with her smile. And this is what you must do for King Pluto."

"Never!" answered Proserpina, looking as miserable as she could. "I shall never smile again till you set me down at my mother's door."

But she might just as well have talked to the wind that whistled past them; for Pluto urged on his horses, and went faster than ever. Proserpina continued to cry out, and screamed so long and so loudly, that her poor little voice was almost screamed away; and when it was nothing but a whisper, she happened to cast her eyes over a great, broad field of waving grain—and whom do you think she saw? Who, but Mother Ceres, making the corn grow, and too busy to notice the golden chariot as it went rattling along. The child mustered all her strength, and gave one more scream, but was out of sight before Ceres had time to turn her head.

King Pluto had taken a road which now began to grow excessively gloomy. It was bordered on each side with rocks and precipices, between which the rumbling of the chariot-wheels was reverberated with a noise like rolling thunder. The trees and bushes that grew in the crevices of the rocks had very dismal foliage; and by and by, although it was hardly noon, the air became obscured with a gray twilight. The black horses had rushed along so swiftly, that they were already beyond the limits of the sunshine. But the duskier it grew, the more did Pluto's visage assume an air of satisfaction. After all, he was not an ill-looking person, especially when he left off twisting his features into a smile that did not belong to them. Proserpina peeped at his face through the gathering dusk, and hoped that he might not be so very wicked as she at first thought him.

"Ah, this twilight is truly refreshing," said King Pluto, "after being so tormented with that ugly and impertinent glare of the sun. How much more agreeable is lamplight or torchlight, more particularly when reflected from diamonds! It will be a magnificent sight when we get to my palace."

"Is it much farther?" asked Proserpina. "And will you carry me back when I have seen it?"

"We will talk of that by and by," answered Pluto. "We are just entering my dominions. Do you see that tall gateway before us? When we pass those gates, we are at home. And there lies my faithful mastiff at the threshold. Cerberus!* Cerberus! Come hither, my good dog!"

So saying, Pluto pulled at the reins, and stopped the chariot right between the tall, massive pillars of the gateway. The mastiff of which he had spoken got up from the threshold, and stood on his hinder legs, so as to put his fore paws on the chariot-wheel. But, my stars, what a strange dog it was! Why, he was a big, rough, ugly-looking monster, with three separate heads, and each of them fiercer than the two others; but, fierce as they were, King Pluto patted them all. He seemed as fond of his three-headed dog as if it had been a sweet little spaniel, with silken ears and curly hair. Cerberus, on the other hand, was evidently rejoiced to see his master,

*Cerberus (sūr'-bēr-əs)

and expressed his attachment, as other dogs do, by wagging his tail at a great rate. Proserpina's eyes being drawn to it by its brisk motion, she saw that this tail was neither more nor less than a live dragon, with fiery eyes, and fangs that had a very poisonous aspect. And while the three-headed Cerberus was fawning so lovingly on King Pluto, there was the dragon tail wagging against its will, and looking as cross and ill-natured as you can imagine, on its own separate account.

"Will the dog bite me?" asked Proserpina, shrinking closer to Pluto. "What an ugly creature he is!"

"Oh, never fear," answered her companion. "He never harms people, unless they try to enter my dominions without being sent for, or to get away when I wish to keep them here. Down Cerberus! Now, my pretty Proserpina, we will drive on."

On went the chariot, and King Pluto seemed greatly pleased to find himself once more in his own kingdom. He drew Proserpina's attention to the rich veins of gold that were to be seen among the rocks, and pointed to several places where one stroke of a pickaxe would loosen a bushel of diamonds. All along the road, indeed, there were sparkling gems, which would have been of inestimable value above ground, but which were here reckoned of the meaner sort, and hardly worth a beggar's stooping for.

Not far from the gateway, they came to a bridge, which seemed to be built of iron. Pluto stopped the chariot, and bade Proserpina look at the stream which was gliding so lazily beneath it. Never in her life had she beheld so torpid, so black, so muddy-looking a

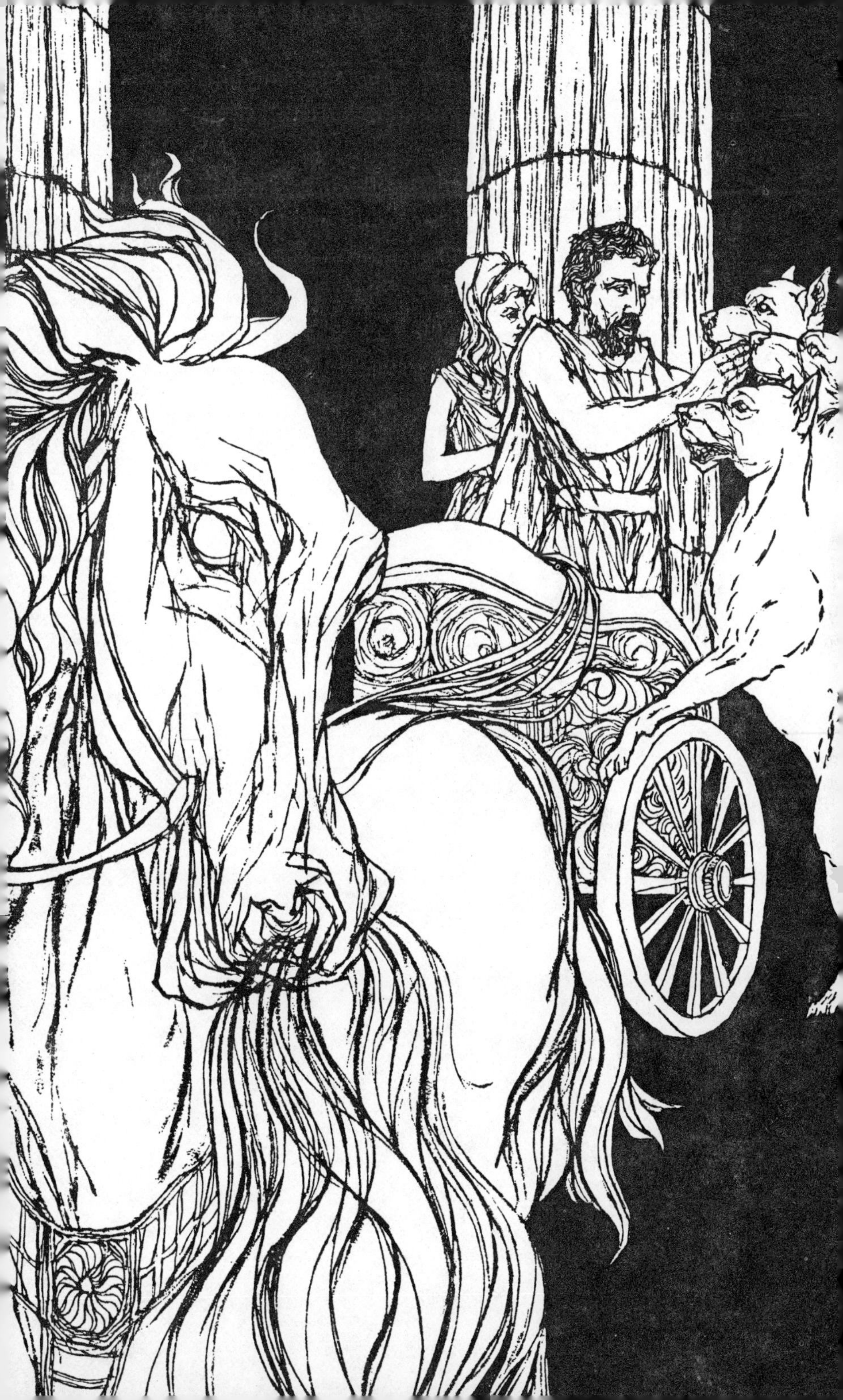

stream: its waters reflected no images of anything that was on the banks, and it moved as sluggishly as if it had quite forgotten which way it ought to flow, and had rather stagnate than flow either one way or the other.

"This is the river Lethe," observed King Pluto. "Is it not a very pleasant stream?"

"I think it a very dismal one," said Proserpina.

"It suits my taste, however," answered Pluto, who was apt to be sullen when anybody disagreed with him. "At all events, its water has one very excellent quality; for a single draught of it makes people forget every care and sorrow that has hitherto tormented them. Only sip a little of it, my dear Proserpina, and you will instantly cease to grieve for your mother, and will have nothing in your memory that can prevent your being perfectly happy in my palace. I will send for some, in a golden goblet, the moment we arrive."

"Oh no, no, no!" cried Proserpina, weeping afresh. "I had a thousand times rather be miserable with remembering my mother, than be happy in forgetting her. That dear, dear mother! I never, never will forget her."

"We shall see," said King Pluto. "You do not know what fine times we will have in my palace. Here we are just at the portal. These pillars are solid gold, I assure you."

He alighted from the chariot, and taking Proserpina in his arms, carried her up a lofty flight of steps into the great hall of the palace. It was splendidly illuminated by means of large precious stones, of various hues, which seemed to burn like so many lamps, and glowed with a hundred-fold radiance all through the vast apartment. And yet there was a kind of gloom in the midst of this enchanted light; nor was there a single object in the hall that was really agreeable to behold, except the little Proserpina herself, a lovely child, with one earthly flower which she had not let fall from her hand. It is my opinion that even King Pluto had never been happy in his palace, and that this was the true reason why he had stolen away Proserpina, in order that he might have something to love, instead of cheating his heart any longer with this tiresome magnificence. And, though he pretended to dislike the sunshine of the upper world, yet the effect of the child's presence, bedimmed as she was by her tears, was as if a faint and watery sunbeam had somehow or other found its way into the enchanted hall.

Pluto now summoned his domestics, and bade them lose no time in preparing a most sumptuous banquet, and above all things, not to fail of setting a golden beaker of the water of Lethe by Proserpina's plate.

"I will neither drink that nor anything else," said Proserpina. "Nor will I taste a morsel of food, even if you keep me forever in your palace."

"I should be sorry for that," replied King Pluto, patting her cheek; for he really wished to be kind, if he had only known how. "You are a spoiled child, I perceive, my little Proserpina; but when you see the nice things which my cook will make for you, your appetite will quickly come again."

Then, sending for the head cook, he gave strict orders that all sorts of delicacies, such as young people are usually fond of, should be set before Proserpina. He had a secret motive in this; for, you are to understand, it is a fixed law, that when persons are carried off to the land of magic, if they once taste any food there, they can never get back to their friends. Now, if King Pluto had been cunning enough to offer Proserpina some fruit, or bread and milk (which was the simple fare to which the child had always been accustomed), it is very probable that she would soon have been tempted to eat it. But he left the matter entirely to his cook, who, like all other cooks, considered nothing fit to eat unless it were rich pastry, or highly seasoned meat, or spiced sweet cakes, —things which Proserpina's mother had never given her, and the smell of which quite took away her appetite, instead of sharpening it.

But my story must now clamber out of King Pluto's dominions, and see what Mother Ceres has been about, since she was bereft of her daughter. We had a glimpse of her, as you remember, half hidden among the waving grain, while the four black steeds were swiftly whirling along the chariot in which her beloved Proserpina was so unwillingly borne away. You recollect, too, the loud scream which Proserpina gave, just when the chariot was out of sight.

Of all the child's outcries, this last shriek was the only one that reached the ears of Mother Ceres. She had mistaken the rumbling of the chariot-wheels for a peal of thunder, and imagined that a shower was coming up, and that it would assist her in making the corn grow. But, at the sound of Proserpina's shriek, she started, and looked about in every direction, not knowing whence it came, but feeling almost certain that it was her daughter's voice. It seemed so unaccountable, however, that the girl should have strayed over so many lands and seas (which she herself could not have traversed without the aid of her winged dragons), that the good Ceres tried to believe that it must be the child of some other parent, and not her own darling Proserpina, who had uttered this lamentable cry. Nevertheless, it troubled her with a vast many tender fears, such as are ready to bestir themselves in every mother's heart, when she finds it necessary to go away from her dear children without leaving them under the care of some maiden aunt, or other such faithful guardian. So she quickly left the field in which she had been so busy; and, as her work was not half done, the grain looked, next day, as if it needed both sun and rain, and as if it were blighted in the ear, and had something the matter with its roots.

The pair of dragons must have had very nimble wings; for, in less than an hour, Mother Ceres had alighted at the door of her home, and found it empty. Knowing, however, that the child was fond of sporting on the seashore, she hastened thither as fast as she could, and there beheld the wet faces of the poor sea-nymphs peeping over a wave. All this while, the good creatures had been waiting on the bank of sponge, and, once every half-minute or so, had popped up their four heads above water, to see if their playmate were yet coming back. When they saw Mother Ceres, they sat down on the crest of the surf wave, and let it toss them ashore at her feet.

"Where is Proserpina?" cried Ceres. "Where is my child? Tell me, you naughty sea-nymphs, have you enticed her under the sea?"

"Oh no, good Mother Ceres," said the innocent sea-nymphs, tossing back their green ringlets, and looking her in the face. "We never should dream of such a thing. Proserpina has been at play with us, it is true; but she left us a long while ago, meaning only to run a little way upon the dry land, and gather some flowers for a wreath. This was early in the day, and we have seen nothing of her since."

Ceres scarcely waited to hear what the nymphs had to say, before she hurried off to make inquiries all through the neighborhood. But nobody told her anything that could enable the poor mother to guess what had become of Proserpina. A fisherman, it is true, had noticed her little footprints in the sand, as he went homeward along the beach with a basket of fish; a rustic had seen the child stooping to gather flowers; several persons had heard either the rattling of chariot-wheels, or the rumbling of distant thunder; and one old woman, while plucking vervain and catnip, had heard a scream, but supposed it to be some childish nonsense, and therefore did not take the trouble to look up. The stupid people! It took them such a tedious while to tell the nothing that they knew, that it was dark night before Mother Ceres found out that she must seek her daughter elsewhere. So she lighted a torch, and set forth, resolving never to come back until Proserpina was discovered.

In her haste and trouble of mind, she quite forgot her car and the winged dragons; or, it may be, she thought that she could follow up the search more thoroughly on foot. At all events, this was the way in which she began her sorrowful journey, holding her torch before her, and looking carefully at every object along the path. And as it happened, she had not gone far before she found one of the magnificent flowers which grew on the shrub that Proserpina had pulled up.

"Ha!" thought Mother Ceres, examining it by torchlight. "Here is mischief in this flower! The earth did not produce it by any help of mine, nor of its own accord. It is the work of enchantment, and is therefore poisonous; and perhaps it has poisoned my poor child."

But she put the poisonous flower in her bosom, not knowing whether she might ever find any other memorial of Proserpina.

All night long, at the door of every cottage and farmhouse, Ceres knocked, and called up the weary laborers to inquire if they had seen her child; and they stood, gaping and half asleep, at the threshold, and answered her pityingly, and besought her to come in and rest. At the portal of every palace, too, she made so loud a summons that the menials hurried to throw open the gate, thinking that it must be some great king or queen, who would demand a banquet for supper and a stately chamber to repose in. And when they saw only a sad and anxious woman, with a torch in her hand and a wreath of withered poppies on her head, they spoke rudely, and sometimes threatened to set the dogs upon her. But nobody had seen Proserpina, nor could give Mother Ceres the least hint which way to seek her. Thus passed the night; and still she continued her search without sitting down to rest, or stopping to take food, or even remembering to put out the torch; although first the rosy dawn, and then the glad light of the morning sun, made its red flame look thin and pale. But I wonder what sort of stuff this torch was made of; for it burned dimly through the day, and, at night, was as bright as ever, and never was extinguished by the rain or wind, in all the weary days and nights while Ceres was seeking for Proserpina.

It was not merely of human beings that she asked tidings of her daughter. In the woods and by the streams, she met creatures of another nature, who used, in those old times, to haunt the pleasant and solitary places, and were very sociable with persons who understood their language and customs, as Mother Ceres did. Sometimes, for instance, she tapped with her finger against the knotted trunk of a majestic oak; and immediately its rude bark would cleave asunder, and forth would step a beautiful maiden, who was the hamadryad* of the oak, dwelling inside of it, and sharing its long life, and rejoicing when its green leaves sported with the breeze. But not one of these leafy damsels had seen Proserpina. Then, going a little farther, Ceres would, perhaps, come to a fountain, gushing out of a pebbly hollow in the earth, and would dabble with her hand in the water. Behold, up through its sandy and pebbly bed, along with the fountain's gush, a young woman with dripping hair would arise, and stand gazing at Mother Ceres, half out of the water, and undulating up and down with its ever-

*hamadryad (ham'-ə-drī'-əd)

restless motion. But when the mother asked whether her poor lost child had stopped to drink out of the fountain, the naiad, with weeping eyes (for these water-nymphs had tears to spare for everybody's grief), would answer, "No!" in a murmuring voice, which was just like the murmur of the stream.

Often, likewise, she encountered fauns, who looked like sunburnt country people, except that they had hairy ears, and little horns upon their foreheads, and the hinder legs of goats, on which they gambolled merrily about the woods and fields. They were a frolicsome kind of creature, but grew as sad as their cheerful dispositions would allow when Ceres inquired for her daughter, and they had no good news to tell. But sometimes she came suddenly upon a rude gang of satyrs, who had faces like monkeys and horses' tails behind them, and who were generally dancing in a very boisterous manner, with shouts of noisy laughter. When she stopped to question them, they would only laugh the louder, and make new merriment out of the lone woman's distress. How unkind of those ugly satyrs! And once, while crossing a solitary sheep-pasture, she saw a personage named Pan, seated at the foot of a tall rock, and making music on a shepherd's flute. He, too, had horns, and hairy ears, and goat's feet; but, being acquainted with Mother Ceres, he answered her question as civilly as he knew how, and invited her to taste some milk and honey out of a wooden bowl. But neither could Pan tell her what had become of Proserpina, any better than the rest of these wild people.

And thus Mother Ceres went wandering about for

nine long days and nights, finding no trace of Proserpina, unless it were now and then a withered flower; and these she picked up and put in her bosom, because she fancied that they might have fallen from her poor child's hand. All day she travelled onward through the hot sun; and at night, again, the flame of the torch would redden and gleam along the pathway, and she continued her search by its light, without ever sitting down to rest.

On the tenth day, she chanced to espy the mouth of a cavern, within which (though it was bright noon everywhere else) there would have been only a dusky twilight; but it so happened that a torch was burning there. It flickered, and struggled with the duskiness, but could not half light up the gloomy cavern with all its melancholy glimmer. Ceres was resolved to leave no spot without a search; so she peeped into the entrance of the cave, and lighted it up a little more, by holding her own torch before her. In so doing, she caught a glimpse of what seemed to be a woman, sitting on the brown leaves of the last autumn, a great heap of which had been swept into the cave by the wind. This woman (if woman it were) was by no means so beautiful as many of her sex; for her head, they tell me, was shaped very much like a dog's, and, by way of ornament, she wore a wreath of snakes around it. But Mother Ceres, the moment she saw her, knew that this was an odd kind of a person, who put all her enjoyment in being miserable, and never would have a word to say to other people, unless they were as melancholy and wretched as she herself delighted to be.

"I am wretched enough now," thought poor Ceres, "to talk with this melancholy Hecate,* were she ten times sadder than ever she was yet."

So she stepped into the cave, and sat down on the withered leaves by the dog-headed woman's side. In all the world, since her daughter's loss, she had found no other companion.

"O Hecate," said she, "if ever you lose a daughter, you will know what sorrow is. Tell me, for pity's sake, have you seen my poor child Proserpina pass by the mouth of your cavern?"

"No," answered Hecate, in a cracked voice, and sighing betwixt every word or two,—"no, Mother Ceres, I have seen nothing of your daughter. But my ears, you must know, are made in such a way that all cries of distress and affright, all over the world are pretty sure to find their way to them; and nine days ago, as I sat in my cave, making myself very miserable, I heard the voice of a young girl, shrieking as if in great distress. Something terrible has happened to the child, you may rest assured. As well as I could judge, a dragon, or some other cruel monster, was carrying her away."

"You kill me by saying so," cried Ceres, almost ready to faint. "Where was the sound, and which way did it seem to go?"

"It passed very swiftly along," said Hecate, "and, at the same time, there was a heavy rumbling of wheels towards the eastward. I can tell you nothing more, except that, in my honest opinion, you will never see your daughter again. The best advice I can give you is, to take up your abode in this cavern, where we will be

*Hecate (hek'-ə-ti)

the two most wretched women in the world."

"Not yet, dark Hecate," replied Ceres. "But do you first come with your torch, and help me to seek for my lost child. And when there shall be no more hope of finding her (if that black day is ordained to come), then, if you will give me room to fling myself down, either on these withered leaves or on the naked rock, I will show you what it is to be miserable. But, until I know that she has perished from the face of the earth, I will not allow myself space even to grieve."

The dismal Hecate did not much like the idea of going abroad into the sunny world. But then she reflected that the sorrow of the disconsolate Ceres would be like a gloomy twilight round about them both, let the sun shine ever so brightly, and that therefore she might enjoy her bad spirits quite as well as if she were to stay in the cave. So she finally consented to go, and they set out together, both carrying torches, although it was broad daylight and clear sunshine. The torchlight seemed to make a gloom; so that the people whom they met along the road could not very distinctly see their figures; and, indeed, if they once caught a glimpse of Hecate, with the wreath of snakes round her forehead, they generally thought it prudent to run away, without waiting for a second glance.

As the pair travelled along in this woe-begone manner, a thought struck Ceres.

"There is one person," she exclaimed, "who must have seen my poor child, and can doubtless tell what has become of her. Why did not I think of him before? It is Phoebus."

"What," said Hecate, "the young man that always sits in the sunshine? Oh, pray do not think of going near him. He is a gay, light, frivolous young fellow, and will only smile in your face. And besides, there is such a glare of the sun about him, that he will quite blind my poor eyes, which I have almost wept away already."

"You have promised to be my companion," answered Ceres. "Come, let us make haste, or the sunshine will be gone, and Phoebus along with it."

Accordingly, they went along in quest of Phoebus, both of them sighing grievously, and Hecate, to say the truth, making a great deal worse lamentation than Ceres; for all the pleasure she had, you know, lay in being miserable, and therefore she made the most of it. By and by, after a pretty long journey, they arrived at the sunniest spot in the whole world. There they beheld a beautiful young man, with long, curling ringlets, which seemed to be made of golden sunbeams; his garments were like light summer clouds; and the expression of his face was so exceedingly vivid, that Hecate held her hands before her eyes, muttering that he ought to wear a black veil. Phoebus (for this was the very person whom they were seeking) had a lyre in his hands, and was making its chords tremble with sweet music; at the same time singing a most exquisite song, which he had recently composed. For, besides a great many other accomplishments, this young man was renowned for his admirable poetry.

As Ceres and her dismal companion approached him, Phoebus smiled on them so cheerfully that Hecate's wreath of snakes gave a spiteful hiss, and Hecate heartily wished herself back in her cave. But as for

Ceres, she was too earnest in her grief either to know or care whether Phoebus smiled or frowned.

"Phoebus!" exclaimed she, "I am in great trouble, and have come to you for assistance. Can you tell me what has become of my dear child Proserpina?"

"Proserpina! Proserpina, did you call her name?" answered Phoebus, endeavoring to recollect; for there was such a continual flow of pleasant ideas in his mind that he was apt to forget what had happened no longer ago than yesterday. "Ah, yes, I remember her now. A very lovely child, indeed. I am happy to tell you, my dear madam, that I did see the little Proserpina not many days ago. You may make yourself perfectly easy about her. She is safe, and in excellent hands."

"Oh, where is my dear child?" cried Ceres, clasping her hands and flinging herself at his feet.

"Why," said Phoebus,—and as he spoke, he kept touching his lyre so as to make a thread of music run in and out among his words,—"as the little damsel was gathering flowers (and she has really a very exquisite taste for flowers) she was suddenly snatched up by King Pluto, and carried off to his dominions. I have never been in that part of the universe; but the royal palace, I am told, is built in a very noble style of architecture, and of the most splendid and costly materials. Gold, diamonds, pearls, and all manner of precious stones will be your daughter's ordinary playthings. I recommend to you, my dear lady, to give yourself no uneasiness. Proserpina's sense of beauty will be duly gratified, and, even in spite of the lack of sunshine, she will lead a very enviable life."

"Hush! Say not such a word!" answered Ceres, indignantly. "What is there to gratify her heart? What are all the splendors you speak of, without affection? I must have her back again. Will you go with me, Phoebus, to demand my daughter of this wicked Pluto?"

"Pray excuse me," replied Phoebus, with an elegant obeisance. "I certainly wish you success, and regret that my own affairs are so immediately pressing that I cannot have the pleasure of attending you. Besides, I am not upon the best of terms with King Pluto. To tell you the truth, his three-headed mastiff would never let me pass the gateway; for I should be compelled to take a sheaf of sunbeams along with me, and those, you know, are forbidden things in Pluto's kingdom."

"Ah, Phoebus," said Ceres, with bitter meaning in her words, "you have a harp instead of a heart. Farewell."

"Will not you stay a moment," asked Phoebus, "and hear me turn the pretty and touching story of Proserpina into extemporary verses?"

But Ceres shook her head, and hastened away, along with Hecate. Phoebus (who, as I have told you, was an exquisite poet) forthwith began to make an ode about the poor mother's grief; and, if we were to judge of his sensibility by this beautiful production, he must have been endowed with a very tender heart. But when a poet gets into the habit of using his heart-strings to make chords for his lyre, he may thrum upon them as much as he will, without any great pain to himself. Accordingly, though Phoebus sang a very sad song, he was as merry all the while as were the sunbeams amid which he dwelt.

Poor Mother Ceres had now found out what had become of her daughter, but was not a whit happier than before. Her case, on the contrary, looked more desperate than ever. As long as Proserpina was above ground there might have been hopes of regaining her. But now that the poor child was shut up within the iron gates of the king of the mines, at the threshold of which lay the three-headed Cerberus, there seemed no possibility of her ever making her escape. The dismal Hecate, who loved to take the darkest view of things, told Ceres that she had better come with her to the cavern, and spend the rest of her life in being miserable. Ceres answered that Hecate was welcome to go back thither herself, but that, for her part, she would wander about the earth in quest of the entrance to King Pluto's dominions. And Hecate took her at her word, and hurried back to her beloved cave, frightening a great many little children with a glimpse of her dog's face, as she went.

Poor Mother Ceres! It is melancholy to think of her, pursuing her toilsome way all alone, and holding up that never-dying torch, the flame of which seemed an emblem of the grief and hope that burned together in her heart. So much did she suffer, that, though her aspect had been quite youthful when her troubles began, she grew to look like an elderly person in a very brief time. She cared not how she was dressed, nor had she ever thought of flinging away the wreath of withered poppies, which she put on the very morning of Proserpina's disappearance. She roamed about in so wild a way, and with her hair so dishevelled, that people took her for some distracted creature, and never dreamed that this was Mother Ceres, who had the oversight of every seed which the husbandman planted. Nowadays, however, she gave herself no trouble about seed-time nor harvest, but left the farmers to take care of their own affairs, and the crops to fade or flourish, as the case might be. There was nothing, now, in which Ceres seemed to feel an interest, unless when she saw children at play, or gathering flowers along the wayside. Then, indeed, she would stand and gaze at them with tears in her eyes. The children, too, appeared to have a sympathy with her grief, and would cluster themselves in a little group about her knees, and look up wistfully in her face; and Ceres, after giving them a kiss all round, would lead them to their homes, and advise their mothers never to let them stray out of sight.

"For if they do," said she, "it may happen to you, as it has to me, that the iron-hearted King Pluto will take a liking to your darlings, and snatch them up in his chariot, and carry them away."

One day, during her pilgrimage in quest of the entrance to Pluto's kingdom, she came to the palace of King Celeus,* who reigned at Eleusis.* Ascending a lofty flight of steps, she entered the portal, and found the royal household in very great alarm about the queen's baby. The infant, it seems, was sickly (being troubled with its teeth, I suppose), and would take no food, and was all the time moaning with pain. The queen—her name was Metanira*—was desirous of finding a nurse; and when she beheld a woman of matronly aspect coming up the palace steps, she thought, in her

*Celeus (sē′-lūs)   *Metanira (met′-ə-nī′-rə)
*Eleusis (el-yōō′-sis)

own mind, that here was the very person whom she needed. So Queen Metanira ran to the door, with the poor wailing baby in her arms, and besought Ceres to take charge of it, or, at least, to tell her what would do it good.

"Will you trust the child entirely to me?" asked Ceres.

"Yes, and gladly too," answered the queen, "if you will devote all your time to him. For I can see that you have been a mother."

"You are right," said Ceres. "I once had a child of my own. Well; I will be the nurse of this poor, sickly boy. But beware, I warn you, that you do not interfere with any kind of treatment which I may judge proper for him. If you do so, the poor infant must suffer for his mother's folly."

Then she kissed the child, and it seemed to do him good; for he smiled and nestled closely into her bosom.

So Mother Ceres set her torch in a corner (where it kept burning all the while), and took up her abode in the palace of King Celeus, as nurse to the little Prince Demophoön.* She treated him as if he were her own child, and allowed neither the king nor the queen to say whether he should be bathed in warm or cold water, or what he should eat, or how often he should take the air, or when he should be put to bed. You would hardly believe me, if I were to tell how quickly the baby prince got rid of his ailments, and grew fat, and rosy, and strong, and how he had two rows of ivory teeth in less time than any other little fellow, before or since. Instead of the palest, and wretchedest, and puniest imp in the world (as his own mother confessed him to be when

*Demophoön (dem-of'-ə-won)

Ceres first took him in charge), he was now a strapping baby, crowing, laughing, kicking up his heels, and rolling from one end of the room to the other. All the good women of the neighborhood crowded to the palace, and held up their hands, in unutterable amazement, at the beauty and wholesomeness of this darling little prince. Their wonder was the greater, because he was never seen to taste any food; not even so much as a cup of milk.

"Pray, nurse," the queen kept saying, "how is it that you make the child thrive so?"

"I was a mother once," Ceres always replied; "and having nursed my own child, I know what other children need."

But Queen Metanira, as was very natural, had a great curiosity to know precisely what the nurse did to her child. One night, therefore, she hid herself in the chamber where Ceres and the little prince were accustomed to sleep. There was a fire in the chimney, and it had now crumbled into great coals and embers, which lay glowing on the hearth, with a blaze flickering up now and then, and flinging a warm and ruddy light upon the walls. Ceres sat before the hearth with the child in her lap, and the firelight making her shadow dance upon the ceiling overhead. She undressed the little prince, and bathed him all over with some fragrant liquid out of a vase. The next thing she did was to rake back the red embers, and make a hollow place among them, just where the backlog had been. At last, while the baby was crowing, and clapping its fat little hands, and laughing in the nurse's face (just as you may have seen your little brother or sister do before going into its warm bath), Ceres suddenly laid him, all naked as he was, in the hollow among the red-hot embers. She then raked the ashes over him, and turned quietly away.

You may imagine, if you can, how Queen Metanira shrieked, thinking nothing less than that her dear child would be burned to a cinder. She burst forth from her hiding-place, and running to the hearth, raked open the fire, and snatched up poor little Prince Demophoön out of his bed of live coals, one of which he was gripping in each of his fists. He immediately set up a grievous cry, as babies are apt to do when rudely startled out of a sound sleep. To the queen's astonishment and joy, she could perceive no token of the child's being injured by the hot fire in which he had lain. She now turned to Mother Ceres, and asked her to explain the mystery.

"Foolish woman," answered Ceres, "did you not promise to intrust this poor infant entirely to me? You little know the mischief you have done him. Had you left him to my care, he would have grown up like a child of celestial birth, endowed with superhuman strength and intelligence, and would have lived forever. Do you imagine that earthly children are to become immortal without being tempered to it in the fiercest heat of the fire? But you have ruined your own son. For though he will be a strong man and a hero in his day, yet, on account of your folly, he will grow old, and finally die, like the sons of other women. The weak tenderness of his mother has cost the poor boy an immortality. Farewell."

Saying these words, she kissed the little prince Demophoön, and sighed to think what he had lost, and took her departure without heeding Queen Metanira, who entreated her to remain, and cover up the child among the hot embers as often as she pleased. Poor baby! He never slept so warmly again.

While she dwelt in the king's palace, Mother Ceres had been so continually occupied with taking care of the young prince, that her heart was a little lightened of its grief for Proserpina. But now, having nothing else to busy herself about, she became just as wretched as before. At length, in her despair, she came to the dreadful resolution that not a stalk of grain, nor a blade of grass, not a potato, nor a turnip, nor any other vegetable that was good for man or beast to eat, should be suffered to grow until her daughter were restored. She even forbade the flowers to bloom, lest somebody's heart should be cheered by their beauty.

Now, as not so much as a head of asparagus ever presumed to poke itself out of the ground, without the especial permission of Ceres, you may conceive what a terrible calamity had here fallen upon the earth. The husbandmen ploughed and planted as usual; but there lay the rich black furrows, all as barren as a desert of sand. The pastures looked as brown in the sweet month of June as ever they did in chill November. The rich man's broad acres and the cottager's small garden-patch were equally blighted. Every little girl's flower-bed showed nothing but dry stalks. The old people shook their white heads, and said that the earth had grown aged like themselves, and was no longer capable of wearing the warm smile of summer on its face. It was really piteous to see the poor, starving cattle and sheep, how they followed behind Ceres, lowing and bleating, as if their instinct taught them to expect help from her; and everybody that was acquainted with her power besought her to have mercy on the human race, and, at all events, to let the grass grow. But Mother Ceres, though naturally of an affectionate disposition, was now inexorable.

"Never," said she. "If the earth is ever again to see any verdure, it must first grow along the path which my daughter will tread in coming back to me."

Finally, as there seemed to be no other remedy, our old friend Quicksilver was sent post haste to King Pluto, in hopes that he might be persuaded to undo the mischief he had done, and to set everything right again, by giving up Proserpina. Quicksilver accordingly made the best of his way to the great gate, took a flying leap right over the three-headed mastiff, and stood at the door of the palace in an inconceivably short time. The servants knew him both by his face and garb; for his short cloak, and his winged cap and shoes, and his snaky staff had often been seen thereabouts in times gone by. He requested to be shown immediately into the king's presence; and Pluto, who heard his voice from the top of the stairs, and who loved to recreate himself with Quicksilver's merry talk, called out to him to come up. And while they settle their business together, we must inquire what Proserpina has been doing ever since we saw her last.

The child had declared, as you may remember, that she would not taste a mouthful of food as long as she should be compelled to remain in King Pluto's palace. How she contrived to maintain her resolution, and at the same time to keep herself tolerably plump and rosy, is more than I can explain; but some young ladies, I am given to understand, possess the faculty of living on air, and Proserpina seems to have possessed it too. At any rate, it was now six months since she left the outside of the earth; and not a morsel, so far as the attendants were able to testify, had yet passed between her teeth. This was the more creditable to Proserpina, inasmuch as King Pluto had caused her to be tempted day after day, with all manner of sweetmeats, and richly preserved fruits, and delicacies of every sort, such as young people are generally most fond of. But her good mother had often told her of the hurtfulness of these things; and for that reason alone, if there had been no other, she would have resolutely refused to taste them.

All this time, being of a cheerful and active disposition, the little damsel was not quite so unhappy as you may have supposed. The immense palace had a thousand rooms, and was full of beautiful and wonderful objects. There was a never-ceasing gloom, it is true, which half hid itself among the innumerable pillars, gliding before the child as she wandered among them, and treading stealthily behind her in the echo of her footsteps. Neither was all the dazzle of the precious stones, which flamed with their own light, worth one gleam of natural sunshine; nor could the most brilliant of the many-colored gems, which Proserpina had for playthings, vie with the simple beauty of the flowers she used to gather. But still, wherever the girl went, among those gilded halls and chambers, it seemed as if she carried nature and sunshine along with her, and as if she scattered dewy blossoms on her right hand and on her left. After Proserpina came, the palace was no longer the same abode of stately artifice and dismal magnificence that it had before been. The inhabitants all felt this, and King Pluto more than any of them.

"My own little Proserpina," he used to say, "I wish you could like me a little better. We gloomy and cloudy-natured persons have often as warm hearts at bottom, as those of a more cheerful character. If you would only stay with me of your own accord, it would make me happier than the possession of a hundred such palaces as this."

"Ah," said Proserpina, "you should have tried to make me like you before carrying me off. And the best thing you can do now is, to let me go again. Then I might remember you sometimes, and think that you were as kind as you knew how to be. Perhaps, too, one day or other, I might come back, and pay you a visit."

"No, no," answered Pluto, with his gloomy smile, "I will not trust you for that. You are too fond of living in the broad daylight, and gathering flowers. What an idle and childish taste that is! Are not these gems, which I have ordered to be dug for you, and which are richer than any in my crown,—are they not prettier than a violet?"

"Not half so pretty," said Proserpina, snatching the gems from Pluto's hand, and flinging them to the other end of the hall. "Oh my sweet violets, shall I never see you again?"

And then she burst into tears. But young people's tears have very little saltness or acidity in them, and do not inflame the eyes so much as those of grown persons; so that it is not to be wondered at if, a few moments afterwards, Proserpina was sporting through the hall almost as merrily as she and the four sea-nymphs had sported along the edge of the surf wave. King Pluto gazed after her, and wished that he, too, was a child. And little Proserpina, when she turned about, and beheld this great king standing in his splendid hall, and looking so grand, and so melancholy, and so lonesome, was smitten with a kind of pity. She ran back to him, and, for the first time in all her life, put her small soft hand in his.

"I love you a little," whispered she, looking up in his face.

"Do you, indeed, my dear child?" cried Pluto, bending his dark face down to kiss her; but Proserpina shrank away from the kiss, for though his features were noble, they were very dusky and grim. "Well, I have not deserved it of you, after keeping you a prisoner for so many months, and starving you, besides. Are you not terribly hungry? Is there nothing which I can get you to eat?"

In asking this question, the king of the mines had a very cunning purpose; for, you will recollect, if Proserpina tasted a morsel of food in his dominions, she would never afterwards be at liberty to quit them.

"No, indeed," said Proserpina. "Your head cook is always baking, and stewing, and roasting, and rolling out paste, and contriving one dish or another, which he imagines may be to my liking. But he might just as well save himself the trouble, poor, fat little man that he is. I have no appetite for anything in the world, unless it were a slice of bread of my mother's own baking, or a little fruit out of her garden."

When Pluto heard this, he began to see that he had mistaken the best method of tempting Proserpina to eat. The cook's made dishes and artificial dainties were not half so delicious, in the good child's opinion, as the simple fare to which Mother Ceres had accustomed her. Wondering that he had never thought of it before, the king now sent one of his trusty attendants, with a large basket, to get some of the finest and juiciest pears, peaches, and plums which could anywhere be found in the upper world. Unfortunately, however, this was during the time when Ceres had forbidden any fruits or vegetables to grow; and, after seeking all over the earth, King Pluto's servant found only a single pomegranate, and that so dried up as to be not worth eating. Nevertheless, since there was no better to be had, he brought this dry, old, withered pomegranate home to the palace, put it on a magnificent golden salver, and carried it up to Proserpina. Now it happened, curiously enough, that, just as the servant was bringing the pomegranate into the back door of the palace, our friend Quicksilver had gone up the front steps, on his errand to get Proserpina away from King Pluto.

As soon as Proserpina saw the pomegranate on the golden salver, she told the servant he had better take it away again.

"I shall not touch it, I assure you," said she. "If I were ever so hungry, I should never think of eating such a miserable, dry pomegranate as that."

"It is the only one in the world," said the servant.

He set down the golden salver, with the wizened pomegranate upon it, and left the room. When he was gone, Proserpina could not help coming close to the table, and looking at this poor specimen of dried fruit with a great deal of eagerness; for, to say the truth, on seeing something that suited her taste, she felt all the six months' appetite taking possession of her at once. To be sure, it was a very wretched-looking pomegranate, and seemed to have no more juice in it than an oyster-shell. But there was no choice of such things in King Pluto's palace. This was the first fruit she had seen there, and the last she was ever likely to see; and unless she ate it up immediately, it would grow drier than it already was, and be wholly unfit to eat.

"At least, I may smell it," thought Proserpina.

So she took up the pomegranate, and applied it to her nose; and, somehow or other, being in such close neighborhood to her mouth, the fruit found its way into that little red cave. Dear me! what an everlasting pity! Before Proserpina knew what she was about, her teeth had actually bitten it, of their own accord. Just as this fatal deed was done, the door of the apartment opened, and in came King Pluto, followed by Quicksilver, who had been urging him to let his little prisoner go. At the first noise of their entrance, Proserpina withdrew the pomegranate from her mouth. But Quicksilver (whose eyes were very keen, and his wits the sharpest that ever anybody had) perceived that the child was a little confused; and seeing the empty salver, he suspected that she had been taking a sly nibble of something or other. As for honest Pluto, he never guessed at the secret.

"My little Proserpina," said the king, sitting down, and affectionately drawing her between his knees, "here is Quicksilver, who tells me that a great many misfortunes have befallen innocent people on account of my detaining you in my dominions. To confess the truth, I myself had already reflected that it was an unjustifiable act to take you away from your good mother. But, then, you must consider, my dear child, that this vast palace is apt to be gloomy (although the precious stones certainly shine very bright), and that I am not of the most cheerful disposition, and that therefore it was a natural thing enough to seek for the society of some merrier creature than myself. I hoped you would take my crown for a plaything, and me—ah, you laugh, naughty Proserpina—me, grim as I am, for a playmate. It was a silly expectation."

"Not so extremely silly," whispered Proserpina. "You have really amused me very much, sometimes."

"Thank you," said King Pluto, rather dryly. "But I can see, plainly enough, that you think my palace a dusky prison, and me the iron-hearted keeper of it. And an iron heart I should surely have, if I could detain you here any longer, my poor child, when it is now six months since you tasted food. I give you your liberty. Go with Quicksilver. Hasten home to your dear mother."

Now, although you may not have supposed it, Proserpina found it impossible to take leave of poor King Pluto without some regrets, and a good deal of compunction for not telling him about the pomegranate. She even shed a tear or two, thinking how lonely and cheerless the great palace would seem to him, with all its ugly glare of artificial light, after she herself,—his one little ray of natural sunshine, whom he had stolen, to be sure, but only because he valued her so much,—after she should have departed. I know not how many kind things she might have said to the disconsolate king of the mines, had not Quicksilver hurried her away.

"Come along quickly," whispered he in her ear, "or his Majesty may change his royal mind. And take care, above all things, that you say nothing of what was brought you on the golden salver."

In a very short time, they had passed the great gateway (leaving the three-headed Cerberus, barking, and yelping, and growling, with threefold din, behind them), and emerged upon the surface of the earth. It was delightful to behold, as Proserpina hastened along, how the path grew verdant behind and on either side of her. Wherever she set her blessed foot, there was at once a dewy flower. The violets gushed up along the wayside. The grass and the grain began to sprout with tenfold vigor and luxuriance, to make up for the dreary months that had been wasted in barrenness. The starved cattle immediately set to work grazing, after their long fast, and ate enormously all day, and got up at midnight to eat more. But I can assure you it was a busy time of year with the farmers, when they found the summer coming upon them with such a rush. Nor must I forget to say that all the birds in the whole world hopped about upon the newly blossoming trees, and sang together in a prodigious ecstasy of joy.

Mother Ceres had returned to her deserted home, and

was sitting disconsolately on the doorstep, with her torch burning in her hand. She had been idly watching the flame for some moments past, when, all at once, it flickered and went out.

"What does this mean?" thought she. "It was an enchanted torch, and should have kept burning till my child came back."

Lifting her eyes, she was surprised to see a sudden verdure flashing over the brown and barren fields, exactly as you may have observed a golden hue gleaming far and wide across the landscape, from the just risen sun.

"Does the earth disobey me?" exclaimed Mother Ceres, indignantly. "Does it presume to be green, when I have bidden it be barren, until my daughter shall be restored to my arms?"

"Then open your arms, dear mother," cried a well-known voice, "and take your little daughter into them."

And Proserpina came running, and flung herself upon her mother's bosom. Their mutual transport is not to be described. The grief of their separation had caused both of them to shed a great many tears; and now they shed a great many more, because their joy could not so well express itself in any other way.

When their hearts had grown a little more quiet, Mother Ceres looked anxiously at Proserpina.

"My child," said she, "did you taste any food while you were in King Pluto's palace?"

"Dearest mother," answered Proserpina, "I will tell you the whole truth. Until this very morning, not a morsel of food had passed my lips. But to-day, they brought me a pomegranate (a very dry one it was, and all shrivelled up, till there was little left of it but seeds and skin), and having seen no fruit for so long a time, and being faint with hunger, I was tempted just to bite it. The instant I tasted it, King Pluto and Quicksilver came into the room. I had not swallowed a morsel; but—dear mother, I hope it was no harm—but six of the pomegranate seeds, I am afraid, remained in my mouth."

"Ah, unfortunate child, and miserable me!" exclaimed Ceres. "For each of those six pomegranate seeds you must spend one month of every year in King Pluto's palace. You are but half restored to your mother. Only six months with me, and six with that good-for-nothing King of Darkness!"

"Do not speak so harshly of poor King Pluto," said Proserpina, kissing her mother. "He has some very good qualities; and I really think I can bear to spend six months in his palace, if he will only let me spend the other six with you. He certainly did very wrong to carry me off; but then, as he says, it was but a dismal sort of life for him, to live in that great gloomy place, all alone; and it has made a wonderful change in his spirits to have a little girl to run up stairs and down. There is some comfort in making him so happy; and so, upon the whole, dearest mother, let us be thankful that he is not to keep me the whole year round."

TALKING ABOUT THE STORY

1. Ceres was the goddess of all growing things; Pluto was king of the underworld where nothing grew.

When Proserpina left the earth, what happened to plants? Why? What season did Proserpina spend with Pluto? with Ceres?
2. Ceres roamed the earth, searching for her daughter. How did Ceres show perseverance and imagination during her search? What other traits did she show?
   The people Ceres met responded to her in different ways, depending on their personalities. How did the sea-nymphs react to Ceres? How did the farmers react? the palace servants? the fauns? the satyrs? Hecate? Phoebus? Quicksilver?
3. What was Pluto's attitude toward Proserpina?
   What personality traits did Proserpina show while she was in his kingdom?
4. Compare Ceres and Proserpina. How were they alike? How were they different?
5. Supernatural objects, beings, and actions were very important in this myth. What quality did they add?
   Were you suspicious of the unusual bush Proserpina found? Why? How did you know Cerberus was a supernatural animal? What magical power was in the water of the river Lethe? Discuss other examples of the supernatural in this story.

WORDS FROM MYTHOLOGY

Panic
   Pan, the Greek god of shepherds, had the horns, feet, and tail of a goat, but the head and shoulders of a

man. He protected the sheep in the fields and enjoyed frisking in the woods. His appearance was so unusual that he created *panic* whenever he emerged unexpectedly before travellers.

Pan also continually played melodies upon reed pipes. Strange noises heard at night in the woods, said to be Pan's pipe playing, also created *panic*.

Did Proserpina *panic* when she saw Pluto? When did Demophoön's mother *panic*? How does a *panicky* crowd behave?

GREEK WORDS IN OUR LANGUAGE

Scholars who study the origins of words are called *philologists*. The root *philo* means "love." *Logos* means "a word." *Philologist* is a Greek word referring to people who are in love with words. Can you discover the meanings of these English words that contain the Greek root *philo*?

What is a *bibliophile*?
What is a *philanthropist*?
What is a *philosopher*?
Do you know a *philatelist*?
What is a *philharmonic* organization?
What is the nickname of *Philadelphia*?

IDEAS FOR WRITING

Nathaniel Hawthorne didn't always tell everything his characters were thinking. It would be interesting to imagine their thoughts.

What do you suppose Cerberus thought of Proserpina? Was he glad when she arrived? Was she healthier than the people he usually saw? Did Cerberus hate her because she took Pluto's attention away from him? Did Cerberus want to visit earth?

Pluto very much wanted Proserpina to stay in Hades. Why? How did he try to persuade her to remain? Why did he fail? How did Pluto feel?

Were the farmers worried about their crops when Ceres stopped the growth of plants? Were they angry with the goddess or did they understand her problem?

What did the sea-nymphs think about and talk about when they returned to their haunts under the water? Did they have a plan to help Ceres find her daughter?

Select an incident from the story and write an account of it as though a different character were thinking. Choose one of the situations you have discussed or another one that you prefer. Or describe some of the delights in Pluto's kingdom. A different person might have liked his realm better than Proserpina did.

adventures of heroes

section 2

LIKE PEOPLE today, the Greeks enjoyed stories of heroes. Greek heroes fended off evil foes at stupendous risks. They struggled against wicked kings. They outwitted fiendish ghouls. They fought carnivorous monsters in hand-to-hand combat. The Greek people told stories about their heroes over and over again.

The story of the adventures of a hero is called a legend. Legendary heroes of any country display the personal qualities most admired by its citizens: bravery, strength, dedication to duty, and fairness to others. The stories tell about men who actually lived, but through the years their adventures and feats have become so exaggerated that the heroes seem larger than life.

Consider this well-known tall tale: A three-pound rainbow trout grows to a four or five pound catch in a fisherman's mind. The bigger fish is more fun to talk about and people enjoy the story. Years later, the man raves about the fifty-pound trout he once hooked.

Hero stories arose in a similar way. The man who slew a fierce animal exaggerated the incident each time he told about it. People added more exciting details to the story as it spread from city to city. Snakes grew into fire-breathing dragons. Powerful opponents became giants. Storytellers combined the adventures of several men into one story. Finally one tremendous hero emerged.

Now you will read about the adventures of heroes—colossal legendary heroes who were the supermen of the Greek world.

One of the great exciting adventures of ancient Greece was the quest for the golden fleece. Only the bravest young men of the day dared volunteer for this hazardous voyage. Jason, the leader of the expedition, needed special courage on the journey, for he and his men would encounter sorcery and other horrors.

BY SALLY BENSON

the golden fleece

In very ancient times there lived in Thessaly a king and queen named Athamas* and Nephele.* They had two children, a boy and a girl. After a time Athamas grew tired of his wife, divorced her and married another. Nephele worried about her children and, not wishing to leave them with a stepmother, took measures to send them away. Mercury came to her aid and gave her a ram with golden fleece on which she put the two children, trusting that the ram would carry them to a place of safety. The ram vaulted into the air with the children on his back and crossed the straits that divide Europe and Asia. Here the girl, whose name was Helle,* slipped from the ram's back and fell into the sea. And thereafter the straits were called the Hellespont.* In modern times, they are called the Dardanelles.* The ram continued his course until he reached the

*Athamas (ath'-ə-məs) *Hellespont (hel'-əs-pont')
*Nephele (nef'-ə-li)   *Dardanelles (där'-də-nelz')
*Helle (hel'-i)

kingdom of Colchis,* on the eastern shore of the Black Sea, where he safely landed the boy Phrixus.* The king of the country, Aeetes,* gladly welcomed the boy, and Phrixus asked that the ram be sacrificed to Jupiter. Its golden fleece was preserved and given to Aeetes. He placed it reverently in a consecrated grove under the care of a dragon who never slept.

There was another kingdom in Thessaly ruled over by a relative of King Athamas. The king, whose name was Aeson,* grew tired of the cares of government and surrendered his crown to his brother Pelias,* on the condition that he should reign only until Aeson's son, Jason,* became of age. When Jason was grown up and came to demand the crown from his uncle, Pelias pretended to be willing to yield it, but suggested that Jason go on some glorious adventure before settling down to the worries of ruling a kingdom. He reminded him that the golden fleece was still in Colchis and that as it was the rightful property of their family, Jason should go in quest of it. The idea excited Jason and he made grand preparations for the expedition. At that time, the only way of navigation known to the Greeks was travel in small boats or canoes hollowed out from the trunks of trees. Jason, realizing that such boats would be too light for the long, hazardous trip, employed Argos to build him a vessel which would carry fifty men. It was considered a gigantic undertaking and took many months. When it was completed, Jason named the ship Argo in honor of the builder, and sent out an invitation to all the adventurous young men in Greece to join him on the expedition. He soon found himself the head of a band

*Colchis (kol'-kis)   *Aeson (ē'-sən)
*Phrixus (frik'-səs)   *Pelias (pē'-li-əs)
*Aeetes (ā-ē'-tēz)   *Jason (jā'-s'n)

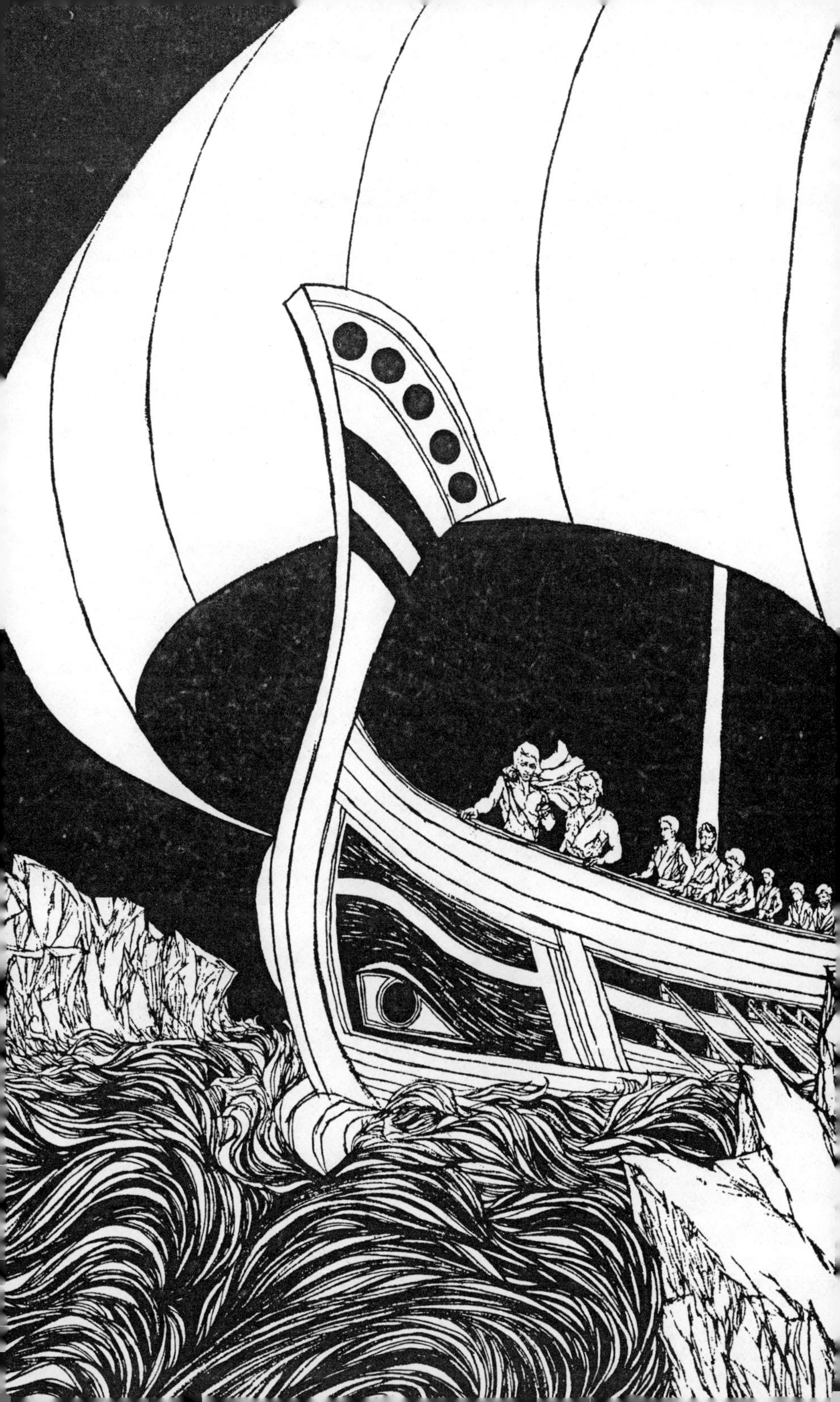

of bold youths, many of whom afterward were renowned among the heroes and demigods of Greece; Hercules, Orpheus* and Nestor were among them. They called themselves the Argonauts.*

The Argo with her crew of heroes left the shores of Thessaly and having stopped for supplies at the island of Lemnos, crossed over to Mysia* and then to Thrace. Here they consulted a wise old man who gave them instructions as to what course to follow. The entrance to the Euxine* Sea was impeded by two small rocky islands. These islands were tossed and heaved about by the sea and occasionally came together, crushing and grinding to atoms any object that might be caught between them. They were called the Symplegades,* or Clashing Islands. The old man told the Argonauts how to pass this dangerous strait; when they reached the islands they released a dove from her cage and watched her as she passed between the rocks in safety. She lost only a few feathers from her tail. Then Jason and his men seized the favorable moment of the rebound, threw all their strength into the oars, and passed swiftly through, though the islands closed behind them and actually grazed their stern. They rowed close to the shore until they landed at the kingdom of Colchis.

Jason went before the king, Aeetes, who consented to give up the golden fleece, if Jason would yoke two fire-breathing bulls to the plough and sow more of the teeth of the dragon which Athena had told Cadmus to slay. Aeetes knew very well that a crop of armed men would spring up who would turn against Jason. The young man agreed to sow the teeth and a time was set for

*Orpheus (or'-fē-əs)   *Euxine (ūk'-sin)
*Argonauts (är'-gə-nôts')   *Symplegades (sim-pleg'-ə-dēz)
*Mysia (mish'-i-ə)

making the experiment. Meanwhile, the Argonauts feasted and reveled.

As preparations were being made for the task, Jason met and fell in love with Medea,* daughter of the king, and asked her to marry him as they stood before the altar of Hecate, goddess of witchcraft and sorcery, who witnessed their oaths. Then Medea, who was skilled in the art of sorcery, gave him a charm which would protect him against the fire-breathing bulls and the weapons of the armed men.

At the appointed time, the people assembled at the grove of Mars and the king assumed his royal seat, while multitudes covered the nearby hillside. The brazen-foot bulls rushed onto the field, breathing fire from their nostrils that burned up grass and bushes as they passed. The sound of their breathing was like the roar of a furnace, and the smoke like that of water upon quicklime. Everybody shrank back at their approach, but Jason walked forth boldly to meet them. His friends turned away in fear for his life. He went near the beasts and soothed them with his voice, patted their necks and adroitly slipped on the yoke. When they were harnessed, he gently guided the plough. The Colchians were amazed. The Greeks shouted for joy. Jason next sowed the dragon's teeth and ploughed them in. And soon the crop of armed men sprang up, but no sooner had they reached the surface than they began to brandish their weapons and rush about Jason. The Argonauts trembled for their leader and even Medea feared her charm might not protect him. For a time Jason kept his assailants at bay with his sword and shield. Then, finding that their numbers were overwhelming, he resorted

*Medea (mi-dē'-ə)

to the charm which Medea had taught him. He seized a stone and threw it into the midst of his foes. They immediately turned their arms against one another and soon there was not one of the dragon's brood left alive. The Greeks cheered their hero and Medea sat proud and happy at her father's side.

Jason, having won the right to the golden fleece, had to pass by the huge dragon to get it. Once more, Medea came to his aid. She gave him a powerful oil which Jason scattered near the monster. At the smell, he stood motionless for a moment, then shut his great eyes that had never been known to close before, turned over on his side, and went fast to sleep.

Jason seized the fleece and with his friends and Medea hastened to the Argo before Aeetes could dispute their departure. They sailed back to Thessaly and Jason delivered the fleece to Pelias and dedicated the Argo to Jupiter.

There was great rejoicing now that the golden fleece had been won for Thessaly, and Jason longed for his father, Aeson, to share in the festivities. But Aeson was old and infirm and could not take part in them. Jason turned to Medea for help. "My spouse," he said, "would that your arts, whose powers have aided me, could do me one more service. Take some of the years from my life and add them to my father's."

Medea replied, "I shall not do it at such a cost, but if my art serves me, his life shall be lengthened without shortening yours."

The next full moon, she went forth all alone, while everyone slept. Not a breath stirred the foliage and all was still. She addressed her incantations to the stars and to the moon; she called on Hecate who represented the darkness and its terrors, and on Tellus,* the goddess of the earth, who produced plants potent for enchantments. She invoked the gods of the woods and caverns, of mountains and valleys, of lakes and rivers, of winds and vapors. As she spoke, the stars shone brighter, and presently a chariot descended through the air, drawn by flying serpents. She stepped into it and was borne aloft to distant regions where strange plants grew. She spent nine days and nine nights selecting a few from the thousands that she saw, and during this time, she did not enter a door, nor did she sleep under a roof, nor speak to any mortal.

She next erected two altars, one to Hecate and the other to Hebe,* goddess of youth, and sacrificed a black sheep to the goddesses, pouring them libations of milk and wine. She begged Pluto and his stolen bride, Proserpina, not to take the old man's life. Then she directed that Aeson should be led forth and she put him to sleep with a potent charm. She laid him on a bed of herbs, like one dead. Throughout these ceremonies, Jason and all the others were kept away so that no profane eyes should look upon her mysteries. With her hair streaming, she moved around the altars three times, dipped flaming twigs in the blood of the sheep and laid them on the altars to burn. She prepared a huge cauldron and in it she put magic herbs, with seeds and flowers of acrid juices, stones from the distant East and sand from the shore of the all-surrounding ocean. She put in hoar frost, gathered by moonlight, a screech owl's head and wings, and the entrails of a wolf. She added fragments of the

*Tellus (tel'-əs)   *Hebe (hē'-bi)

shells of tortoises, and the livers of stags, the head and beak of a crow that outlives nine generations of men. These with many other things so weird that they had no name she boiled together, stirring them up with a wild olive branch. And when the branch was taken out of the mixture, it instantly became green! Before long it was covered with leaves and a plentiful growth of young olives. As the liquor boiled and bubbled, grass sprouted on the ground where the liquid fell.

When all was ready, Medea cut the old man's throat and let out all his blood and poured into his mouth and into the wound the juices of her cauldron. Slowly his hair and beard changed from white to a rich dark black; he lost his paleness and his body grew vigorous and robust. Aeson was amazed when he awoke to find that he looked as he had forty years ago.

When Pelias's daughters saw what Medea had done for Aeson, they begged her to restore youth to their own father. But, Medea, remembering that Pelias had kept Jason from ruling his kingdom while he sent him on the dangerous quest for the golden fleece, only pretended to agree. She prepared her cauldron as before, and at her request an old sheep was brought and plunged into it. Very soon a bleating was heard in the kettle, and a lamb jumped forth and ran frisking away to the meadows. The daughters of Pelias saw this experiment and were delighted, and appointed a time for their father to undergo the same operation. But Medea put water and a few simple herbs in it, instead. And in the night, she and the daughters entered the bedchamber of the old king while he and his guards slept soundly. The daughters stood by the bedside, but hesitated to cut their father's throat until Medea jeered at them for their irresolution. Turning away their heads, they struck random blows. Pelias, starting from his sleep, cried out, "My daughters, what are you doing? Will you kill your father?"

Their hearts failed them and the weapons fell from their hands, but Medea struck him a final blow. His daughters carried him to the altar and placed him in the cauldron, and Medea hastened to depart in her serpent-drawn chariot. She escaped, but was to live to repent her evil deed. Jason turned away from her in disgust and desired to marry Creusa,* princess of Corinth. Medea, enraged at his ingratitude after the help she had given him, sent a poisoned robe as a gift to the princess and then set fire to the palace. She escaped once more in her serpent-drawn chariot and fled to Athens, where she married King Aegeus,* the father of Theseus.*

TALKING ABOUT THE STORY

1. What was Pelias's reason for sending Jason on the quest? Did you believe Pelias was sincere? Why?
2. A Greek hero needed more than sheer strength to endure his trials. In what endeavors was Jason successful? What contributed to his success?

    Tell which of the following terms best describe Jason: cunning, powerful, timid, adventurous. Why? Think of other words that characterize him.

*Creusa (krē-ōō′-sə)
*Ægeus (ē′-jōōs)
*Theseus (thē′-sōōs)

3. Medea, one of the two witches in Greek mythology, appealed to the gods for help. Which gods did she invoke? How did each assist her?
4. Did Jason's feelings about Medea change? How did he feel when she first helped him? as the story progressed?

EXPRESSIONS FROM MYTHOLOGY

Suppose you read that a man had "sown dragon's teeth." Why does this expression mean he has done something that will cause trouble?

GREEK WORDS IN OUR LANGUAGE

1. The Greek root *naus* means ship. What is a *nautical* trip? The *Argonauts* were Greek adventurers. How are *astronauts* like *Argonauts*? How are they different? What is a *cosmonaut*?
2. The Greek root *thermo* means "heat." Many English words have been formed from this word root. A *thermometer*, for example, measures the body's heat. What is a *thermos* bottle? a *thermostat*? *thermonuclear* energy?
3. The Greek word *kyklos*, meaning "circle" or "wheel" became "cycle" in English. A *bicycle* is a vehicle with two wheels. What is a *unicycle*? a *tricycle*? How does a *motorcycle* operate?

IDEAS FOR WRITING

Some descriptions are so vivid that you actually feel a part of them. Could you visualize Medea concocting the witch's brew? What could you see? smell? hear?

Now imagine details about the dragon guarding the fleece. What color were its teeth? eyes? hair? How did it move? breathe? Were bones of its victims lying around?

What were the fire-breathing bulls like?

Describe either animal so that a reader could picture it in his mind.

Evil monsters terrorized the road to Athens. Periphetes clubbed men to death. Sinis murdered travelers by tying their arms to two bent-over pine trees, and letting the trees go. Sciron, Kerkuon, and Procrustes were equally demonic.

Theseus, on his way to meet his father for the first time, killed every one of the fiends singlehandedly and arrived in Athens a hero. Little did he know that a death struggle with the most ferocious monster of all awaited him.

BY CHARLES KINGSLEY

theseus and the minotaur

Theseus stayed with his father all the winter; and when the spring equinox drew near, all the Athenians grew sad and silent, and Theseus saw it, and asked the reason; but no one would answer him a word.

Then he went to his father, and asked him: but Ægeus turned away his face and wept.

"Do not ask, my son, beforehand, about evils which must happen: it is enough to have to face them when they come."

And when the spring equinox came, a herald came to Athens, and stood in the market, and cried, "O people and King of Athens, where is your yearly tribute?" Then a great lamentation arose throughout the city. But Theseus stood up to the herald, and cried, "And who are you, dog-faced,

133

who dare demand tribute here? If I did not reverence your herald's staff, I would brain you with this club."

And the herald answered proudly, for he was a grave and ancient man, "Fair youth, I am not dog-faced or shameless; but I do my master's bidding, Minos* the King of hundred-citied Crete,* the wisest of all kings on earth. And you must be surely a stranger here, or you would know why I come, and that I come by right."

"I am a stranger here. Tell me, then, why you come."

"To fetch the tribute which King Ægeus promised to Minos, and confirmed his promise with an oath. For Minos conquered all this land, and Megara* which lies to the east, when he came hither with a great fleet of ships, enraged about the murder of his son. For his son Androgeos* came hither to the Panathenaic* games, and overcame all the Greeks in the sports, so that the people honoured him as a hero. But when Ægeus saw his valour, he envied him, and feared lest he should join the sons of Pallas, and take away the sceptre from him. So he plotted against his life, and slew him basely, no man knows how or where. Some say that he waylaid him by Oinoe,* on the road which goes to Thebes; and some that he sent him against the bull of Marathon, that the beast might kill him. But Ægeus says that the young men killed him from envy, because he had conquered them in the games. So Minos came hither and avenged him, and would not depart till this land had promised him tribute, seven youths and seven maidens every year, who go with me in a black-sailed ship, till they come to hundred-citied Crete."

*Minos (mī'-nəs)
*Crete (krēt)
*Megara (meg'-ə-rə)
*Androgeos (an-drō'-je-əs)
*Panathenaic (pan'-ə-thē'-nē-ək)
*Oinoe (ē-nō'-ə)

And Theseus ground his teeth together, and said, "Wert thou not a herald, I would kill thee for saying such things of my father: but I will go to him, and know the truth." So he went to his father, and asked him; but he turned away his head and wept, and said, "Blood was shed in the land unjustly, and by blood it is avenged. Break not my heart by questions; it is enough to endure in silence."

Then Theseus groaned inwardly, and said, "I will go myself with these youths and maidens, and kill Minos upon his royal throne."

But Ægeus shrieked, and cried, "You shall not go, my son, the light of my old age, to whom alone I look to rule this people, after I am dead and gone. You shall not go, to die horribly, as those youths and maidens die; for Minos thrusts them into a labyrinth, which Daedalos* made for him among the rocks,—Daedalos the renegade, the accursed, the pest of this his native land. From that labyrinth no one can escape, entangled in his winding ways, before they meet the Minotaur* the monster, who feeds upon the flesh of men. There he devours them horribly, and they never see this land again."

Then Theseus grew red, and his ears tingled, and his heart beat loud in his bosom. And he stood awhile like a tall stone pillar, on the cliffs above some hero's grave; and at last he spoke, "Therefore all the more I will go with them, and slay the accursed beast. Have I not slain all evil-doers and monsters, that I might free this land? Where are Periphetes,* and Sinis,* and Kerkuon,* and Phaia* the wild sow? Where are the fifty sons of Pallas?

*Daedalos (ded'-ə-ləs)
*Minotaur (min'-ə-tôr')
*Periphetes (pĕr-if'-ə-tēz)
*Sinis (sī'-nəs)
*Kerkuon (ker'-koo-ən)
*Phaia (fā'-yə)

And this Minotaur shall go the road which they have gone, and Minos himself, if he dare stay me."

"But how will you slay him, my son? For you must leave your club and your armour behind, and be cast to the monster, defenceless and naked like the rest."

And Theseus said, "Are there no stones in that labyrinth; and have I not fists and teeth? Did I need my club to kill Kerkuon, the terror of all mortal men?"

Then Ægeus clung to his knees; but he would not hear; and at last he let him go, weeping bitterly, and said only this one word, "Promise me but this, if you return in peace, though that may hardly be: take down the black sail of the ship, (for I shall watch for it all day upon the cliffs,) and hoist instead a white sail, that I may know afar off that you are safe."

And Theseus promised, and went out, and to the market-place where the herald stood, while they drew lots for the youths and maidens, who were to sail in that doleful crew. And the people stood wailing and weeping, as the lot fell on this one and on that: but Theseus strode into the midst, and cried, "Here is a youth who needs no lot. I myself will be one of the seven."

And the herald asked in wonder, "Fair youth, know you whither you are going?"

And Theseus said, "I know. Let us go down to the black-sailed ship."

So they went down to the black-sailed ship, seven maidens, and seven youths, and Theseus before them all, and the people following them lamenting. But Theseus whispered to his companions, "Have hope, for the monster is not immortal. Where are Periphetes, and Sinis, and Sciron, and all whom I have slain?" Then their hearts were comforted a little: but they wept as they went on board, and the cliffs of Sunium rang, and all the isles of the Ægean Sea, with the voice of their lamentation, as they sailed on toward their deaths in Crete.

And at last they came to Crete, and to Cnossus,* beneath the peaks of Ida, and to the palace of Minos the great king, to whom Zeus himself taught laws. So he was the wisest of all mortal kings, and conquered all the Ægean isles; and his ships were as many as the seagulls, and his palace like a marble hill. And he sat among the pillars of the hall, upon his throne of beaten gold, and around him stood the speaking statues which Daedalos had made by his skill. For Daedalos was the most cunning of all Athenians, and he first invented the plumb-line, and the auger, and glue, and many a tool with which wood is wrought. And he first set up masts in ships, and yards, and his son made sails for them: but Perdix his nephew excelled him; for he first invented the saw and its teeth, copying it from the backbone of a fish; and invented, too, the chisel, and the compasses, and the potter's wheel which moulds the clay. Therefore Daedalos envied him, and hurled him headlong from the temple of Athene: but the Goddess pitied him (for she loves the wise), and changed Perdix into a partridge, which flits forever about the hills. And Daedalos fled to Crete, to Minos, and worked for him many a year, till he did a shameful deed, at which the sun hid his face on high.

*Cnossus (nos'-əs)

Then he fled from the anger of Minos, he and Icaros* his son having made themselves wings of feathers, and fixed the feathers with wax. So they flew over the sea toward Sicily; but Icaros flew too near the sun; and the wax of his wings was melted, and he fell into the Icarian Sea. But Daedalos came safe to Sicily, and there wrought many a wondrous work; for he made for King Cocalos* a reservoir, from which a great river watered all the land, and a castle and a treasury on a mountain, which the giants themselves could not have stormed; and in Selinos* he took the steam which comes up from the fires of Ætna, and made of it a warm bath of vapour, to cure the pains of mortal men; and he made a honeycomb of gold, in which the bees came and stored their honey, and in Egypt he made the forecourt of the temple of Hephaistos in Memphis, and a statue of himself within it, and many another wondrous work. And for Minos he made statues which spoke and moved, and the temple of the sea goddess, Britomartis,* and the dancing-hall of Minos's daughter, Ariadne,* which he carved of fair white stone. And in Sardinia he worked for Hercules' nephew, Iölaos,* and in many a land beside, wandering up and down forever with his cunning, unlovely and accursed by men.

But Theseus stood before Minos, and they looked each other in the face. And Minos bade take them to prison, and cast them to the monster one by one, that the death of Androgeos might be avenged. Then Theseus cried, "A boon, O Minos. Let me be thrown first to the beast. For I came hither for that very purpose, of my own will, and not by lot."

*Icaros (ik'-ə-rəs)
*Cocalus (kō'-kə-ləs)
*Selinos (sə-lē'-nəs)
*Britomartis (brit'-ō-mär'-tis)
*Ariadne (ar'-i-ad'-ni)
*Iölaos (i'-ō-lā'-əs)

"Who art thou, then, brave youth?"

"I am the son of him whom of all men thou hatest most, Ægeus the king of Athens, and I am come here to end this matter."

And Minos pondered awhile, looking steadfastly at him, and he thought, "The lad means to atone by his own death for his father's sin;" and he answered at last mildly, "Go back in peace, my son. It is a pity that one so brave should die."

But Theseus said, "I have sworn that I will not go back till I have seen the monster face to face."

And at that Minos frowned, and said, "Then thou shalt see him; take the madman away."

And they led Theseus away into the prison, with the other youths and maids.

But Ariadne, Minos's daughter, saw him, as she came out of her white stone hall; and she loved him for his courage and his majesty, and said, "Shame that such a youth should die!" And by night she went down to the prison, and told him all her heart; and said, "Flee down to your ship at once, for I have bribed the guards before the door. Flee, you and all your friends, and go back in peace to Greece; and take me, take me with you! For I dare not stay after you are gone; for my father will kill me miserably, if he knows what I have done."

And Theseus stood silent awhile; for he was astonished and confounded by her beauty: but at last he said, "I cannot go home in peace, till I have seen and slain this Minotaur, and avenged the deaths of the youths and maidens, and put an end to the terrors of my land."

"And will you kill the Minotaur? How, then?"

"I know not, nor do I care: but he must be strong if he be too strong for me."

Then she loved him all the more, and said, "But when you have killed him, how will you find your way out of the labyrinth?"

"I know not, neither do I care: but it must be a strange road, if I do not find it out before I have eaten up the monster's carcase."

Then she loved him all the more, and said,

"Fair youth, you are too bold; but I can help you, weak as I am. I will give you a sword, and with that, perhaps, you may slay the beast; and a clue of thread, and by that, perhaps, you may find your way out again. Only promise me, that if you escape safe, you will take me home with you to Greece; for my father will surely kill me, if he knows what I have done."

Then Theseus laughed, and said, "Am I not safe enough now?" And he hid the sword in his bosom, and rolled up the clue in his hand; and then he swore to Ariadne, and fell down before her, and kissed her hands and her feet; and she wept over him a long while, and then went away; and Theseus lay down and slept sweetly.

And when the evening came, the guards came in and led him away to the labyrinth.

And he went down into that doleful gulf, through winding paths among the rocks, under caverns, and arches, and galleries, and over heaps of fallen stone. And he turned on the left hand, and on the right hand, and went up and down, till his head was dizzy; but all

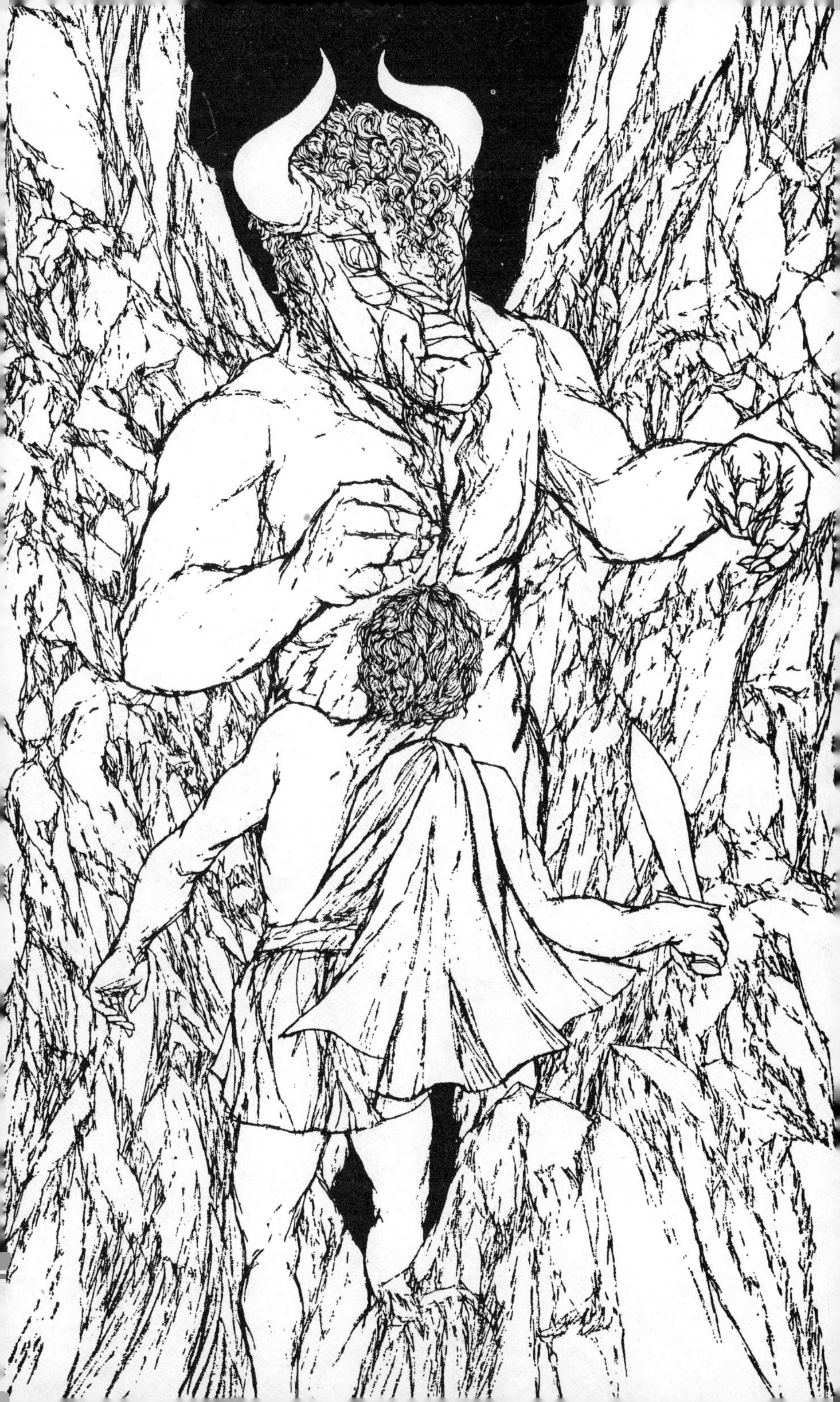

the while he held his clue. For when he went in he had fastened it to a stone, and left it to unroll out of his hand as he went on; and it lasted him till he met the Minotaur, in a narrow chasm between black cliffs.

And when he saw him he stopped awhile, for he had never seen so strange a beast. His body was a man's; but his head was the head of a bull; and his teeth were the teeth of a lion; and with them he tore his prey. And when he saw Theseus he roared, and put his head down, and rushed right at him.

But Theseus stepped aside nimbly, and as he passed by, cut him in the knee; and ere he could turn in the narrow path, he followed him, and stabbed him again and again from behind, till the monster fled bellowing wildly; for he had never before felt a wound. And Theseus followed him at full speed, holding the clue of thread in his left hand.

Then on, through cavern after cavern, under dark ribs of sounding stone, and up rough glens and torrent-beds, among the sunless roots of Ida, and to the edge of the eternal snow, went they, the hunter and the hunted, while the hills bellowed to the monster's bellow.

And at last Theseus came up with him, where he lay panting on a slab among the snow, and caught him by the horns, and forced his head back, and drove the keen sword through his throat.

Then he turned, and went back limping and weary, feeling his way down by the clue of thread, till he came to the mouth of that doleful place; and saw waiting for him, whom but Ariadne!

And he whispered, "It is done!" and showed her the sword; and she laid her finger on her lips, and led him to the prison, and opened the doors, and set all the prisoners free, while the guards lay sleeping heavily; for she had silenced them with wine.

Then they fled to their ship together, and leapt on board, and hoisted up the sail; and the night lay dark around them, so that they passed through Minos's ships, and escaped all safe to Naxos;* and there Ariadne became Theseus's wife.

aftermath

Theseus never took his bride, Ariadne, back to Athens. According to one story Theseus abandoned her at the island of Naxos and Dionysus later married her. Another story tells that Dionysus forced Theseus to give Ariadne to him.

At any rate, Theseus forgot his promise to Ægeus; he did not replace the black sail with a white one. When Ægeus saw the black flag he thought the Minotaur had devoured Theseus. Ægeus, in despair, threw himself over the cliffs. The sea in which he perished has been known as the Ægean Sea ever since.

Theseus performed noble deeds all his life and eventually became the most beloved hero of Athens.

TALKING ABOUT THE STORY

1. " 'Blood was shed in the land unjustly, and by blood it is avenged.' " What did Ægeus mean when he spoke these words?
2. Did you respect King Minos? Why?

*Naxos (nak'-sos)

3. Greek heroes depended on courage, strength, cunning, and help from gods and mortals in their adventures. What did Theseus depend on? Did he rely more on his own resources or those of others? Explain.
4. Have you ever heard someone exaggerate an experience in telling about it? How did you know that the truth had been stretched?

   Some of the events in the story you have just read were based on fact. Other parts of the story were exaggerated. Which things in the story could have been inspired by actual events? Which parts of the story were exaggerated?

WORDS FROM MYTHOLOGY

Labyrinth

Theseus twisted and turned his way through the passageway of the labyrinth. Do any of the activities or games you know remind you of the labyrinth?

IDEAS FOR WRITING

1. If you had been one of the fourteen doomed Athenians, how would you have felt on the voyage to Crete? as you entered the labyrinth? when you saw the Minotaur? Describe your thoughts and feelings.
2. Ariadne's plans helped save Theseus. But suppose Medea had been there and had helped Theseus. Would she have given him a magic potion to drug the Minotaur? a charm to hypnotize him? How else might she have helped Theseus? Write about how Medea might have aided Theseus.

the labours of hercules

When Hercules was only a baby, he killed two deadly snakes with his bare hands. He grew up to be so brave that the Olympians themselves once asked for his help in battle. It is no wonder that Hercules was the most famous Greek hero.

BY REX WARNER

Hercules* suffered much during his life, but after his death he became a god. His mother was Alcmena,* his father was Jupiter, and he was the strongest of all the heroes who lived in his time.

All through his life he was pursued by the hatred and jealousy of Juno* who tried to destroy him even in his cradle. She sent two great snakes to attack the sleeping baby, but Hercules awoke, grasped their necks in his hands and strangled them both.

Before he was eighteen he had done many famous deeds in the country of Thebes, and Creon, the king, gave him his daughter in marriage. But he could not long escape the anger of Juno, who afflicted him with a sudden madness, so that he did not know what he was doing and in a fit of frenzy killed both his wife and his children. When he came to his

146   *Hercules (hūr′-kyōō-lēz′)   *Juno (jōō′-nō)
         *Alcmena (alk-mē′-ni)

senses, in horror and shame at what he had done, he visited the great cliffs of Delphi,* where the eagles circle all day and where Apollo's oracle is. There he asked how he could be purified of his sin and he was told by the oracle that he must go to Mycenae and for twelve years obey all the commands of the cowardly king Eurystheus,* his kinsman. It seemed a hard and cruel sentence, but the oracle told him also, that at the end of many labours he would be received among the gods.

Hercules therefore departed to the rocky citadel of Mycenae that looks down upon the blue water of the bay of Argos.* He was skilled in the use of every weapon, having been educated, like Jason was, by the wise centaur* Chiron.* He was tall and immensely powerful. When Eurystheus saw him he was both terrified of him and jealous of his great powers. He began to devise labours that would seem impossible, yet Hercules accomplished them all.

First Hercules was ordered to destroy and to bring back to Mycenae the lion of Nemea* which for long had ravaged all the countryside to the north. Hercules took his bow and arrows, and, in the forest of Nemea, cut himself a great club, so heavy that a man nowadays could hardly lift it. This club he carried ever afterwards as his chief weapon.

He found that his arrows had no effect on the tough skin of the lion, but, as the beast sprang at him, he half-stunned it with his club, then closing in with it, he seized it by the throat and killed it with his bare hands. They say that when he carried back on his shoulders to Mycenae the body of the huge beast, Eurystheus fled in

*Delphi (del'-fī) *centaur (sen'-tôr)
*Eurystheus (yōō-ris'-thūs) *Chiron (kī'-ron)
*Argos (är'-gos) *Nemea (nē'-mi-ə)

terror and ordered Hercules never again to enter the gates of the city, but to wait outside until he was told to come in. Eurystheus also built for himself a special strong room of brass into which he would retire if he was ever again frightened by the power and valiance of Hercules. Hercules himself took the skin of the lion and made it into a cloak which he wore ever afterwards, sometimes with the lion's head covering his own head like a cap, sometimes with it slung backwards over his shoulders.

The next task given to Hercules by Eurystheus was to destroy a huge water snake, called the Hydra,* which lived in the marshes of Argos, was filled with poison and had fifty venomous heads. Hercules, with his friend and companion, the young Iolaus, set out from Mycenae and came to the great cavern, sacred to Pan, which is a holy place in the hills near Argos. Below this cavern a river gushes out of the rock. Willows and plane-trees surround the source and the brilliant green of grass. It is the freshest and most delightful place. But, as the river flows downwards to the sea, it becomes wide and shallow, extending into pestilential marshes, the home of stinging flies and mosquitoes. In these marshes they found the Hydra, and Hercules, with his great club, began to crush the beast's heads, afterwards cutting them off with his sword. Yet the more he laboured, the more difficult his task became. From the stump of each head that he cut off two other heads, with forked and hissing tongues, immediately sprang. Faced with an endless and increasing effort, Hercules was at a loss what to do. It seemed to him that heat might prove more powerful than cold

*Hydra (hī'-drə)

steel, and he commanded Iolaus to burn the root of each head with a red-hot iron immediately it was severed from the neck. This plan was successful. The heads no longer sprouted up again, and soon the dangerous and destructive animal lay dead, though still writhing in the black marsh water among the reeds. Hercules cut its body open and dipped his arrows in the blood. Henceforward these arrows would bring certain death, even if they only grazed the skin, so powerful was the Hydra's poison.

Eurystheus next ordered Hercules to capture and bring back alive a stag, sacred to Diana and famous for its great fleetness of foot, which lived in the waste mountains and forests, and never yet had been approached in the chase. For a whole year Hercules pursued this animal, resting for the hours of darkness and pressing on next day in its tracks. For many months he was wholly out-distanced; valleys and forests divided him from his prey. But at the end of the year the stag, weary of the long hunt, could run no longer. Hercules seized it in his strong hands, tied first its forelegs and then its hind legs together, put the body of the beast, with its drooping antlered head, over his neck, and proceeded to return to the palace of King Eurystheus. However, as he was on his way through the woods, he was suddenly aware of a bright light in front of him, and, in the middle of the light he saw standing a tall woman or, as he immediately recognized, a goddess, grasping in her hands a bow and staring at him angrily with her shining eyes. He knew at once that this was the archer goddess Diana, she who had once turned the hunter,

Actaeon,* into a stag and who now was enraged at the loss of this other stag which was sacred to her. Hercules put his prey on the ground and knelt before the goddess. "It was through no desire of my own," he said, "that I have captured this noble animal. What I do is done at the command of my father Jupiter and of the oracle of your brother Apollo at Delphi." The goddess listened to his explanation, smiled kindly on him and allowed him to go on his way, when he had promised that, once the stag had been carried to Eurystheus, it would be set free again in the forests that it loved. So Hercules accomplished this third labour.

He was not, however, to be allowed to rest. Eurystheus now commanded him to go out to the mountains of Erymanthus* and bring back the great wild boar that for long had terrorized all the neighbourhood. So Hercules set out once more and on his way he passed the country where the centaurs had settled. The manners of the centaurs were rude and rough. When the centaur Pholus* offered Hercules some of their best wine to drink, the other centaurs became jealous. Angry words led to blows, and soon Hercules was forced to defend himself with his club and with his arrows, the poison of which not only caused death, but also the most extreme pain. Soon he scattered his enemies in all directions, driving them over the plains and rocks. Some he dashed to the ground with his club; others, wounded by the poisoned arrows, lay writhing in agony, or kicking their hooves in the air. Some took refuge in the house of the famous centaur Chiron, who had been schoolmaster to Hercules and who, alone among the centaurs, was immortal. As he pursued

*Actaeon (ak-tē′-ən) *Pholus (fō′-ləs)
*Erymanthus (er′-i-man′-thəs)

his enemies to this good centaur's house, shooting arrows at them as he went, Hercules, by an unhappy accident, wounded Chiron himself. Whether it was because of grief that his old pupil had so injured him, or whether it was because of the great pain of the wound, Chiron prayed to Jupiter that his immortality should be taken away from him. Jupiter granted his prayer. The good centaur died, but he was set in Heaven in a constellation of stars which is still called either Sagittarius* or else The Centaur.

Hercules mourned the sad death of his old master. Then he went on to Erymanthus. It was winter and he chased the great boar up to the deep snow in the passes of the mountains. The animal's short legs soon grew weary of ploughing through the stiff snow and Hercules caught it up when it was exhausted and panting in a snowdrift. He bound it firmly and slung the great body over his back. They say that when he brought it to Mycenae, Eurystheus was so frightened at the sight of the huge tusks and flashing eyes that he hid for two days in the brass hiding place that he had had built for him.

The next task that Hercules was ordered to do would have seemed to anyone impossible. There was a king of Elis* called Augeas,* very rich in herds of goats and cattle. His stables, they say, held three thousand oxen and for ten years these stables had never been cleaned. The dung and muck stood higher than a house, hardened and caked together. The smell was such that even the herdsmen, who were used to it, could scarcely bear to go near. Hercules was now ordered to clean these stables, and, going to Elis, he first asked the king to promise him the

*Sagittarius (saj'-i-târ'-i-əs) *Augeas (ô-jē'-əs)
*Elis (ē'-lis)

tenth part of his herds if he was successful in his task. The king readily agreed, and Hercules made the great river Alpheus* change his course and come foaming and roaring through the filthy stables. In less than a day all the dirt was cleared and rolled away to the sea. The river then went back to its former course and, for the first time in ten years, the stone floors and walls of the enormous stables shone white and clean.

Hercules then asked for his reward, but King Augeas, claiming that he had performed the task not with his own hands, but by a trick, refused to give it to him. He even banished his own son who took the side of Hercules and reproached his father for not keeping his promise. Hercules then made war on the kingdom of Elis, drove King Augeas out and put his son on the throne. Then, with his rich reward, he returned to Mycenae, ready to undertake whatever new task was given him by Eurystheus.

Again he was ordered to destroy creatures that were harmful to men. This time they were great birds, like cranes or storks, but much more powerful, which devoured human flesh and lived around the black waters of the Stymphalian* lake. In the reeds and rocky crags they lived in huge numbers and Hercules was at a loss how to draw them from their hiding places. It was the goddess Minerva who helped him by giving him a great rattle of brass. The noise of this rattle drove the great birds into the air in throngs. Hercules pursued them with his arrows, which rang upon their horny beaks and legs but stuck firm in the bodies that tumbled one after

*Alpheus (al-fē′-əs)
*Stymphalian (stim-fā′-li-ən)

the other into the lake. The whole brood of these monsters was entirely destroyed and now only ducks and harmless water-fowl nest along the reedy shores.

Hercules had now accomplished six of his labours. Six more remained. After the killing of the Stymphalian birds he was commanded to go to Crete and bring back from there alive a huge bull which was laying the whole island waste. Bare-handed and alone he grappled with this bull, and, once again, when he brought the animal back into the streets of Mycenae, Eurystheus fled in terror at the sight both of the hero and of the great beast which he had captured.

From the southern sea Hercules was sent to the north to Thrace, over which ruled King Diomedes,* a strong and warlike prince who savagely fed his famous mares on human flesh. Hercules conquered the king in battle and gave his body to the very mares which had so often fed upon the bodies of the king's enemies. He brought the mares back to King Eurystheus, who again was terrified at the sight of such fierce and spirited animals. He ordered them to be taken to the heights of Mount Olympus and there be consecrated to Jupiter. But Jupiter had no love for these unnatural creatures, and, on the rocky hill-sides, they were devoured by lions, wolves, and bears.

Next Hercules was commanded to go to the country of the Amazons,* the fierce warrior women, and bring back the girdle of their queen Hippolyte.* Seas and mountains had to be crossed, battles to be fought; but Hercules in the end accomplished the long journey and

*Diomedes (di'-ə-mē'-dēz)   *Hippolyte (hi-pol'-i-tə)
*Amazons (am'-ə-zonz')

the dangerous task. Later, as is well known, Hippolyte became the wife of Theseus of Athens and bore him an ill-fated son, Hippolytus.

Hercules had now travelled in the south, the north and the east. His tenth labour was to be in the far west, beyond the country of Spain, in an island called Erythia.* Here lived the giant Geryon,* a great monster with three bodies and three heads. With his herdsman, and his two-headed dog, called Orthrus, he looked after huge flocks of oxen, and, at the command of Eurystheus, Hercules came into his land to lift the cattle and to destroy the giant. On his way, at the very entrance to the Atlantic he set up two great marks, ever afterwards to be known by sailors and called the Pillars of Hercules. Later, as he wandered through rocks and over desert land, he turned his anger against the Sun itself, shooting his arrows at the great god Phoebus Apollo. But Phoebus pitied him in his thirst and weariness. He sent him a golden boat, and in this boat Hercules crossed over to the island of Erythia. Here he easily destroyed both watchdog and herdsman, but fought for long with the great three-bodied giant before he slew him, body after body. Then he began to drive the cattle over rivers and mountains and deserts from Spain to Greece. As he was passing through Italy he came near the cave where Cacus,* a son of Vulcan, who breathed fire out of his mouth, lived solitary and cruel, since he killed all strangers and nailed their heads, dripping with blood, to the posts at the entrance of his rocky dwelling. While Hercules was resting, with the herds all round him, Cacus

*Erythia (er-i-thē′-ə)   *Cacus (ka′-kus)
*Geryon (jêr′-i-ən)

came out of his cave and stole eight of the best animals of the whole herd. He dragged them backwards by their tails, so that Hercules should not be able to track them down.

When Hercules awoke from his rest, he searched far and wide for the missing animals, but, since they had been driven into the deep recesses of Cacus's cave, he was unable to find them. In the end he began to go on his way with the rest of the herd, and, as the stolen animals heard the lowing of the other cattle, they too began to low and bellow in their rocky prison. Hercules stopped still, and soon out of the cave came the fire-breathing giant, prepared to defend the fruits of his robbery and anxious to hang the head of Hercules among his other disgusting trophies. This, however, was not to be. The huge limbs and terrible fiery breath of Cacus were of no avail against the hero's strength and fortitude. Soon, with a tremendous blow of his club, he stretched out Cacus dead on the ground. Then he drove the great herd on over mountains and plains, through forests and rivers to Mycenae.

Hercules' next labour again took him to the far west. He was commanded by Eurystheus to fetch him some of the golden apples of the Hesperides.* These apples grew in a garden west even of the land of Atlas.* Here the sun shines continually, but always cool well-watered trees of every kind give shade. All flowers and fruits that grow on earth grow here, and fruit and flowers are always on the boughs together. In the centre of the garden is the orchard where golden apples gleam among

*Hesperides (hes-per'-ə-dēz')
*Atlas (at'-ləs)

the shining green leaves and the flushed blossom. Three nymphs, the Hesperides, look after this orchard, which was given by Jupiter to Juno as a wedding present. It is guarded also by a great dragon that never sleeps, and coils its huge folds around the trees. No one except the gods knows exactly where this beautiful and remote garden is, and it was to this unknown place that Hercules was sent.

He was helped by Minerva and by the nymphs of the broad river Po in Italy. These nymphs told Hercules where to find Nereus,* the ancient god of the sea, who knew the past, the present and the future. "Wait for him," they said, "until you find him asleep on the rocky shore, surrounded by his fifty daughters. Seize hold of him tightly and do not let go until he answers your question. He will, in trying to escape you, put on all kinds of shapes. He will turn to fire, to water, to a wild beast or to a serpent. You must not lose your courage, but hold him all the tighter, and, in the end, he will come back to his own shape and will tell you what you want to know."

Hercules followed their advice. As he watched along the sea god's shore he saw, lying on the sand, half in and half out of the sea, with seaweed trailing round his limbs, the old god himself. Around him were his daughters, the Nereids,* some riding on the backs of dolphins, some dancing on the shore, some swimming and diving in the deeper water. As Hercules approached, they cried out shrilly at the sight of a man. Those on land leaped back into the sea; those in the sea swam further from the shore. But their cries did not awake their father till

*Nereus (nêr'-ōos)   *Nereid (nêr'-i-id)

Hercules was close to him and able to grip him firmly in his strong hands. Immediately the old god felt the hands upon him, his body seemed to disappear into a running stream of water; but Hercules felt the body that he could not see, and did not relax his grasp. Next it seemed that his hands were buried in a great pillar of fire; but the fire did not scorch the skin and Hercules could still feel the aged limbs through the fire. Then it was a great lion with wide-open jaws that appeared to be lying and raging on the sands; then a bear, then a dragon. Still Hercules clung firmly to his prisoner, and in the end he saw again the bearded face and seaweed-dripping limbs of old Nereus. The god knew for what purpose Hercules had seized him, and he told him the way to the garden of the Hesperides.

It was a long and difficult journey, but at the end of it Hercules was rewarded. The guardian nymphs (since this was the will of Jupiter) allowed him to pick from the pliant boughs two or three of the golden fruit. The great dragon bowed its head to the ground at their command and left Hercules unmolested. He brought back the apples to Eurystheus, but soon they began to lose that beautiful sheen of gold that had been theirs in the western garden. So Minerva carried them back again to the place from which they came, and then once more they glowed with their own gold among the other golden apples that hung upon the trees.

Now had come the time for the twelfth and last of the labours that Hercules did for his master Eurystheus. This labour would seem to anyone by far the hardest; for the hero was commanded to descend into the lower world, and bring back with him from the kingdom of Proserpine the terrible three-headed watch-dog Cerberus.

Hercules took the dark path which before him had been trodden only by the Greek heroes Orpheus and Theseus and Pirithous.* Orpheus had returned. Theseus and Pirithous, for their wicked attempt to kidnap Proserpine, were still imprisoned.

Hercules passed the Furies,* undaunted by the frightful eyes beneath the writhing serpents of their hair. He passed the great criminals, Sisyphus,* Tantalus and the rest of those condemned to remain in the lower world. He passed by his friend, the unhappy Theseus, who was sitting immovably fixed to a rock, and he came at last into the terrible presence of black Pluto himself, who sat on his dark throne with his young wife Proserpine beside him. To the King and Queen of the Dead Hercules explained the reason of his coming. "Go," said Pluto, "and, so long as you use no weapon, but only your bare hands, you may take my watch-dog Cerberus to the upper air."

Hercules thanked the dreadful king for giving him the permission which he had asked. Then he made one more request which was that Theseus, who had sinned only by keeping his promise to his friend, might be allowed to return again to life. This, too, was granted him. Theseus rose to his feet again and accompanied the hero to the entrance of Hell, where the huge dog Cerberus, with his three heads and his three deep baying voices, glared savagely at the intruders. Even this tremendous animal proved no match for Hercules, who with his vice-like grip stifled the breath in two of the

*Pirithous (pī-rith'-ō-əs)   *Sisyphus (sis'-ə-fəs)
*Furies (fyōō'-rēz)

shaggy throats, then lifted the beast upon his shoulders and began to ascend again, Theseus following close behind, the path that leads to the world of men. They say that when he carried Cerberus to Mycenae, Eurystheus fled in terror to another city and was now actually glad that Hercules had completed what might seem to have been twelve impossible labours. Cerberus was restored to his place in Hell and never again visited the upper world. Nor did Hercules ever go down to the place of the dead, since, after further trials, he was destined to live among the gods above.

TALKING ABOUT THE STORY

1. Hercules performed twelve seemingly impossible labors. Why? In completing these feats he depended on strength, stamina, intellect, or assistance from others. How did he accomplish each task?

Lion of Nemea	Cretan Bull
Hydra	Mares of Thrace
Diana's Stag	Amazons
Wild Boar	Geryon
Augean Stables	Golden Apples
Stymphalian Birds	Cerberus

   What personal quality did Hercules rely on most?

2. What kind of person was King Eurystheus? Would he have undertaken a mission as dangerous as any of those on which he sent Hercules?

3. If Hercules lived today, what occupations might he be likely to follow? Explain.

EXPRESSIONS FROM MYTHOLOGY

The labors of Hercules have become very famous. Perhaps you have heard people comparing their own problems to those of Hercules, saying something like this: "Rescuing the drowning man was a Herculean task!" Perhaps you have read descriptions like these, based on the labors of Hercules: "A runner as fleet as Diana's stag"; "as threatening as Geryon." Try making up your own expressions based on Hercules' labors.

GREEK WORDS IN OUR LANGUAGE

Dino comes from the Greek word for "terrible." *Saurus* means "lizard" in Greek. So a *dinosaur* is a terrible lizard. What would a *titanosaurus* be? a *gigantosaurus*?

IDEAS FOR WRITING

Hercules ridded the ancient Greek countryside of monsters and captured wondrous animals and objects. If Hercules lived today, what might his labors be? Would he overcome tidal waves? unsnarl traffic jams? What are some other modern "monsters"? Describe an adventure of a modern Hercules.

Perseus pledged himself to an encounter with the deadly Gorgons, three scaly dragon-sisters with wriggling snakes instead of hair. So hideous were these monsters that any man who saw them turned to stone. Nevertheless, Perseus embarked upon the terrifying mission.

BY NATHANIEL HAWTHORNE

PERSEUS

Perseus* was the son of Danaë,* who was the daughter of a king. And when Perseus was a very little boy, some wicked people put his mother and himself into a chest, and set them afloat upon the sea. The wind blew freshly, and drove the chest away from the shore, and the uneasy billows tossed it up and down; while Danaë clasped her child closely to her bosom, and dreaded that some big wave would dash its foamy crest over them both. The chest sailed on, however, and neither sank nor was upset; until, when night was coming, it floated so near an island that it got entangled in a fisherman's nets, and was drawn out high and dry upon the sand. The island was called Seriphus,* and it was reigned over by King Polydectes,* who happened to be the fisherman's brother.

This fisherman, I am glad to tell you, was an exceedingly humane and upright man. He showed great kindness to Danaë and her little

*Perseus (pūr'-sūs)   *Seriphus (ser'-ə-fəs)
*Danaë (dan'-i-ē')   *Polydectes (pol'-ə-dek'-tēz)

boy; and continued to befriend them, until Perseus had grown to be a handsome youth, very strong and active, and skillful in the use of arms. Long before this time, King Polydectes had seen the two strangers—the mother and her child—who had come to his dominions in a floating chest. As he was not good and kind like his brother the fisherman, but extremely wicked, he resolved to send Perseus on a dangerous enterprise in which he would probably be killed, and then to do some great mischief to Danaë herself, so this bad-hearted king spent a long while in considering what was the most dangerous thing that a young man could possibly undertake to perform. At last, having hit upon an enterprise that promised to turn out as fatally as he desired, he sent for the youthful Perseus.

The young man came to the palace, and found the king sitting upon his throne.

"Perseus," said King Polydectes, smiling craftily upon him, "you are grown up a fine young man. You and your good mother have received a great deal of kindness from myself as well as from my worthy brother the fisherman, and I suppose you would not be sorry to repay some of it."

"Please your majesty," answered Perseus, "I would willingly risk my life to do so."

"Well, then," continued the king, still with a cunning smile on his lips, "I have a little adventure to propose to you; and, as you are a brave and enterprising youth, you will doubtless look upon it as a great piece of good luck to have so rare an opportunity of distinguishing yourself. You must know, my good Perseus, I think of getting married to the beautiful Princess Hippodamia;* and it

*Hippodamia (hip'-ə-dā'-mi-ə)

is customary, on these occasions, to make the bride a present of some far-fetched and elegant curiosity. I have been a little perplexed, I must honestly confess, where to obtain anything likely to please a princess of her exquisite taste. But, this morning, I flatter myself, I have thought of precisely the article."

"And can I assist your Majesty in obtaining it?" cried Perseus, eagerly.

"You can, if you are as brave a youth as I believe you to be," replied King Polydectes, with the utmost graciousness of manner. "The bridal gift which I have set my heart on presenting to the beautiful Hippodamia is the head of the Gorgon Medusa* with the snaky locks; and I depend on you, my dear Perseus, to bring it to me. So, as I am anxious to settle affairs with the princess, the sooner you go in quest of the Gorgon, the better I shall be pleased."

"I will set out to-morrow morning," answered Perseus.

"Pray do so, my gallant youth," rejoined the king. "And, Perseus, in cutting off the Gorgon's head, be careful to make a clean stroke, so as not to injure its appearance. You must bring it home in the very best condition, in order to suit the exquisite taste of the beautiful Princess Hippodamia."

Perseus left the palace, but was scarcely out of hearing before Polydectes burst into a laugh; being greatly amused, wicked king that he was, to find how readily the young man fell into the snare. The news quickly spread abroad that Perseus had undertaken to cut off the head of Medusa with the snaky locks. Everybody was

*Medusa (mə-doo′-sə)

rejoiced; for most of the inhabitants of the island were as wicked as the king himself, and would have liked nothing better than to see some enormous mischief happen to Danaë and her son. The only good man in this unfortunate island of Seriphus appears to have been the fisherman. As Perseus walked along, therefore, the people pointed after him, and made mouths, and winked to one another, and ridiculed him as loudly as they dared.

"Ho, ho!" cried they; "Medusa's snakes will sting him soundly."

Now, there were three Gorgons alive at that period; and they were the most strange and terrible monsters that had ever been seen since the world was made, or that have been seen in after days, or that are likely to be seen in all time to come. I hardly know what sort of creature or hobgoblin to call them. They were three sisters, and seem to have borne some distant resemblance to women, but were really a very frightful and mischievous species of dragon. It is, indeed, difficult to imagine what hideous beings these three sisters were. Why, instead of locks of hair, if you can believe me, they had each of them a hundred enormous snakes, growing on their heads, all alive, twisting, wriggling, curling, and thrusting out their venomous tongues, with forked stings at the end! The teeth of the Gorgons were terribly long tusks; their hands were made of brass; and their bodies were all over scales, which, if not iron, were something as hard and impenetrable. They had wings, too, and exceedingly splendid ones, I can assure you; for every feather in them was pure, bright, glittering, burnished gold, and they looked very dazzlingly, no doubt, when the Gorgons were flying about in the sunshine.

But when people happened to catch a glimpse of their glittering brightness, aloft in the air, they seldom stopped to gaze, but ran and hid themselves as speedily as they could. You will think, perhaps, that they were afraid of being stung by the serpents that served the Gorgons instead of hair,—or of having their heads bitten off by their ugly tusks,—or of being torn all to pieces by their brazen claws. Well, to be sure, these were some of the dangers, but by no means the greatest, nor the most difficult to avoid. For the worst thing about these abominable Gorgons was, that, if once a poor mortal fixed his eyes full upon one of their faces, he was certain, that very instant, to be changed from warm flesh and blood into cold and lifeless stone!

Thus, as you will easily perceive, it was a very dangerous adventure that the wicked King Polydectes had contrived for this innocent young man. Perseus himself, when he had thought over the matter, could not help seeing that he had very little chance of coming safely through it, and that he was far more likely to become a stone image than to bring back the head of Medusa with the snaky locks. For not to speak of other difficulties, there was one which it would have puzzled an older man than Perseus to get over. Not only must he fight with and slay this golden-winged, iron-scaled, long-tusked, brazen-clawed, snaky-haired monster, but he must do it with his eyes shut, or, at least, without so much as a glance at the enemy with whom he was contending. Else, while his arm was lifted to strike, he would stiffen into stone, and stand with that uplifted arm for centuries, until time, and the wind and weather, should crumble him quite away. This would be a very sad thing to befall a young man who wanted to perform a great many brave deeds, and to enjoy a great deal of happiness, in this bright and beautiful world.

So disconsolate did these thoughts make him, that Perseus could not bear to tell his mother what he had undertaken to do. He therefore took his shield, girded on his sword, and crossed over from the island to the mainland, where he sat down in a solitary place, and hardly refrained from shedding tears.

But, while he was in this sorrowful mood, he heard a voice close behind him.

"Perseus," said the voice, "why are you sad?"

He lifted his head from his hands, in which he had hidden it, and, behold! all alone as Perseus had supposed himself to be, there was a stranger in the solitary place. It was a brisk, intelligent, and remarkably shrewd-looking young man, with a cloak over his shoulders, an odd sort of cap on his head, a strangely twisted staff in his hand, and a short and very crooked sword hanging by his side. He was exceedingly light and active in his figure, like a person much accustomed to gymnastic exercises, and well able to leap or run. Above all, the stranger had such a cheerful, knowing, and helpful aspect (though it was certainly a little mischievous, into the bargain), that Perseus could not help feeling his spirits grow livelier as he gazed at him. Besides, being really a courageous youth, he felt greatly ashamed that anybody should have found him with tears in his eyes, like a timid little school-boy, when, after all, there might be no occasion for despair. So Perseus wiped his eyes, and answered the stranger pretty briskly, putting on as brave a look as he could.

"I am not so very sad," said he, "only thoughtful about an adventure that I have undertaken."

"Oho!" answered the stranger. "Well, tell me all about it, and possibly I may be of service to you. I have helped a good many young men through adventures that looked difficult enough beforehand. Perhaps you may have heard of me. I have more names than one; but the name of Quicksilver suits me as well as any other. Tell me what the trouble is, and we will talk the matter over, and see what can be done."

The stranger's words and manner put Perseus into quite a different mood from his former one. He resolved to tell Quicksilver all his difficulties, since he could not easily be worse off than he already was, and, very possibly, his new friend might give him some advice that would turn out well in the end. So he let the stranger know, in few words, precisely what the case was,—how that King Polydectes wanted the head of Medusa with the snaky locks as a bridal gift for the beautiful Princess Hippodamia, and how that he had undertaken to get it for him, but was afraid of being turned into stone.

"And that would be a great pity," said Quicksilver, with his mischievous smile. "You would make a very handsome marble statue, it is true, and it would be a considerable number of centuries before you crumbled away; but, on the whole, one would rather be a young man for a few years, than a stone image for a great many."

"Oh, far rather!" exclaimed Perseus, with the tears again standing in his eyes. "And, besides, what would my dear mother do, if her beloved son were turned into a stone?"

"Well, well, let us hope that the affair will not turn out so very badly," replied Quicksilver, in an encouraging tone. "I am the very person to help you if anybody can. My sister and myself will do our utmost to bring you safe through the adventure, ugly as it now looks."

"Your sister?" repeated Perseus.

"Yes, my sister," said the stranger. "She is very wise, I promise you; and as for myself, I generally have all my wits about me, such as they are. If you show yourself bold and cautious, and follow our advice, you need not fear being a stone image yet awhile. But, first of all, you must polish your shield, till you can see your face in it as distinctly as in a mirror."

This seemed to Perseus rather an odd beginning of the adventure; for he thought it of far more consequence that the shield should be strong enough to defend him from the Gorgon's brazen claws, than that it should be bright enough to show him the reflection of his face. However, concluding that Quicksilver knew better than himself, he immediately set to work and scrubbed the shield with so much diligence and good-will, that it very quickly shone like the moon at harvest-time. Quicksilver looked at it with a smile, and nodded his approbation. Then, taking off his own short and crooked sword, he girded it about Perseus, instead of the one which he had before worn.

"No sword but mine will answer your purpose," observed he; "the blade has a most excellent temper, and will cut through iron and brass as easily as through the slenderest twig. And now we will set out. The next thing is to find the Three Gray Women, who will tell us where to find the Nymphs."

"The Three Gray Women!" cried Perseus, to whom this seemed only a new difficulty in the path of his adventure; "pray who may the Three Gray Women be? I never heard of them before."

"They are three very strange old ladies," said Quicksilver, laughing. "They have but one eye among them, and only one tooth. Moreover, you must find them out by starlight, or in the dusk of the evening; for they never show themselves by the light either of the sun or moon."

"But," said Perseus, "why should I waste my time with these Three Gray Women? Would it not be better to set out at once in search of the terrible Gorgons?"

"No, no," answered his friend. "There are other things to be done, before you can find your way to the Gorgons. There is nothing for it but to hunt up these old ladies; and when we meet with them, you may be sure that the Gorgons are not a great way off. Come, let us be stirring."

Perseus, by this time, felt so much confidence in his companion's sagacity, that he made no more objections, and professed himself ready to begin the adventure immediately. They accordingly set out, and walked at a pretty brisk pace; so brisk, indeed, that Perseus found it rather difficult to keep up with his nimble friend Quicksilver. To say the truth, he had a singular idea that Quicksilver was furnished with a pair of winged shoes, which, of course, helped him along marvellously. And then, too, when Perseus looked sideways at him, out of the corner of his eyes, he seemed to see wings on the side of his head; although, if he turned a full gaze, there were no such things to be perceived, but only an odd kind of cap. But, at all events, the twisted staff was evidently a great convenience to Quicksilver, and enabled him to proceed so fast, that Perseus, though a remarkably active young man, began to be out of breath.

"Here!" cried Quicksilver, at last,—for he knew well enough, rogue that he was, how hard Perseus found it to keep pace with him,—"take you the staff, for you need it a great deal more than I. Are there no better walkers than yourself in the island of Seriphus?"

"I could walk pretty well," said Perseus, glancing slyly at his companion's feet, "if I had only a pair of winged shoes."

"We must see about getting you a pair," answered Quicksilver.

But the staff helped Perseus along so bravely, that he no longer felt the slightest weariness. In fact, the stick seemed to be alive in his hand, and to lend some of its life to Perseus. He and Quicksilver now walked onward at their ease, talking very sociably together; and Quicksilver told so many pleasant stories about his former adventures, and how well his wits had served him on various occasions, that Perseus began to think him a very wonderful person. He evidently knew the world; and nobody is so charming to a young man as a friend who has that kind of knowledge. Perseus listened the more eagerly, in the hope of brightening his own wits by what he heard.

At last, he happened to recollect that Quicksilver had spoken of a sister, who was to lend her assistance in the adventure which they were now bound upon.

"Where is she?" he inquired. "Shall we not meet her soon?"

"All at the proper time," said his companion. "But this sister of mine, you must understand, is quite a different sort of character from myself. She is very grave and prudent, seldom smiles, never laughs, and makes it a rule not to utter a word unless she has something particularly profound to say. Neither will she listen to any but the wisest conversation."

"Dear me!" ejaculated Perseus; "I shall be afraid to say a syllable."

"She is a very accomplished person, I assure you," continued Quicksilver, "and has all the arts and sciences at her fingers' ends. In short, she is so immoderately wise, that many people call her wisdom personified. But, to tell you the truth, she has hardly vivacity enough for my taste; and I think you would scarcely find her so pleasant a travelling companion as myself. She has her good points, nevertheless; and you will find the benefit of them, in your encounter with the Gorgons."

By this time it had grown quite dusk. They were now come to a very wild and deserted place, overgrown with shaggy bushes, and so silent and solitary that nobody seemed ever to have dwelt or journeyed there. All was waste and desolate, in the gray twilight, which grew every moment more obscure. Perseus looked about him, rather disconsolately, and asked Quicksilver whether they had a great deal farther to go.

"Hist! hist!" whispered his companion. "Make no noise! This is just the time and place to meet the Three Gray Women. Be careful that they do not see you before you see them; for, though they have but a single eye among the three, it is as sharp-sighted as half a dozen common eyes."

"But what must I do," asked Perseus, "when we meet them?"

Quicksilver explained to Perseus how the Three Gray Women managed with their one eye. They were in the habit, it seems, of changing it from one to another, as if it had been a pair of spectacles, or—which would have suited them better—a quizzing-glass. When one of the three had kept the eye a certain time, she took it out of the socket and passed it to one of her sisters, whose turn it might happen to be, and who immediately clapped it into her own head, and enjoyed a peep at the visible world. Thus it will be easily understood that only one of the Three Gray Women could see, while the other two were in utter darkness; and, moreover, at the instant when the eye was passing from hand to hand, neither of the poor old ladies was able to see a wink. I have heard of a great many strange things in my day, and have witnessed not a few; but none, it seems to me, that can compare with the oddity of these Three Gray Women, all peeping through a single eye.

So thought Perseus, likewise, and was so astonished that he almost fancied his companion was joking with him, and that there were no such old women in the world.

"You will soon find whether I tell the truth or no," observed Quicksilver. "Hark! hush hist! hist! There they come, now!"

Perseus looked earnestly through the dusk of the evening, and there, sure enough, at no great distance off, he descried the Three Gray Women. The light being so faint, he could not well make out what sort of figures they were; only he discovered that they had long gray hair; and, as they came nearer, he saw that two of them had but the empty socket of an eye in the middle of their foreheads. But, in the middle of the third sister's forehead, there was a very large, bright, and piercing eye, which sparkled like a great diamond in a ring; and so penetrating did it seem to be, that Perseus could not help thinking it must possess the gift of seeing in the darkest midnight just as perfectly as at noonday. The sight of three persons' eyes was melted and collected into that single one.

Thus the three old dames got along about as comfortably, upon the whole, as if they could all see at once. She who chanced to have the eye in her forehead led the other two by the hands, peeping sharply about her all the while; insomuch that Perseus dreaded lest she should see right through the thick clump of bushes behind which he and Quicksilver had hidden themselves. My stars! it was positively terrible to be within reach of so very sharp an eye!

But, before they reached the clump of bushes, one of the Three Gray Women spoke.

"Sister! Sister Scarecrow!" cried she, "you have had the eye long enough. It is my turn now!"

"Let me keep it a moment longer, Sister Nightmare," answered Scarecrow. "I thought I had a glimpse of something behind that thick bush."

"Well, and what of that?" retorted Nightmare peevishly. "Can't I see into a thick bush as easily as yourself? The eye is mine as well as yours; and I know the use of it as well as you, or may be a little better. I insist upon taking a peep immediately!"

But here the third sister, whose name was Shakejoint, began to complain, and said that it was her turn to have the eye, and that Scarecrow and Nightmare wanted to keep it all to themselves. To end the dispute, old Dame Scarecrow took the eye out of her forehead, and held it forth in her hand.

"Take it, one of you," cried she, "and quit this foolish quarrelling. For my part, I shall be glad of a little thick darkness. Take it quickly, however, or I must clap it into my own head again!"

Accordingly, both Nightmare and Shakejoint put out their hands, groping eagerly to snatch the eye out of the hand of Scarecrow. But being both alike blind, they could not easily find where Scarecrow's hand was; and Scarecrow, being just now as much in the dark as Shakejoint and Nightmare, could not at once meet either of their hands, in order to put the eye into it. Thus (as you will see, with half an eye, my wise little auditors), these good old dames had fallen into a strange perplexity. For, though the eye shone and glistened like a star, as Scarecrow held it out, yet the Gray Women caught not the least glimpse of its light, and were all three in utter darkness, from too impatient a desire to see.

Quicksilver was so much tickled at beholding Shakejoint and Nightmare both groping for the eye, and each finding fault with Scarecrow and one another, that he could scarcely help laughing aloud. "Now is your time!" he whispered to Perseus. "Quick, quick! before they can clap the eye into either of their heads. Rush out upon the old ladies, and snatch it from Scarecrow's hand!"

In an instant, while the Three Gray Women were still scolding each other, Perseus leaped from behind the clump of bushes, and made himself master of the prize. The marvellous eye, as he held it in his hand, shone very brightly, and seemed to look up into his face with a knowing air, and an expression as if it would have winked, had it been provided with a pair of eyelids for that purpose. But the Gray Women knew nothing of what had happened; and, each supposing that one of her sisters was in possession of the eye, they began their quarrel anew. At last, as Perseus did not wish to put these respectable dames to greater inconvenience than was really necessary, he thought it right to explain the matter.

"My good ladies," said he, "pray do not be angry with one another. If anybody is in fault, it is myself; for I have the honor to hold your very brilliant and excellent eye in my own hand!"

"You! you have our eye! And who are you?" screamed the Three Gray Women, all in a breath; for they were terribly frightened, of course, at hearing a strange voice, and discovering that their eyesight had got into the hands of they could not guess whom. "Oh, what shall we do, sisters? what shall we do? We are all in the dark! Give us our eye! Give us our one, precious, solitary eye! You have two of your own! Give us our eye!"

"Tell them," whispered Quicksilver to Perseus, "that they shall have back the eye as soon as they direct you where to find the Nymphs who have the flying slippers, the magic wallet, and the helmet of darkness."

"My dear, good, admirable old ladies," said Perseus, addressing the Gray Women, "there is no occasion for putting yourselves into such a fright. I am by no means a bad young man. You shall have back your eye, safe and sound, and as bright as ever, the moment you tell me where to find the Nymphs."

"The Nymphs! Goodness me! sisters, what Nymphs does he mean?" screamed Scarecrow. "There are a great many Nymphs, people say; some that go a-hunting in the woods, and some that live inside of trees, and some that have a comfortable home in fountains of water. We know nothing at all about them. We are three unfortunate old souls, that go wandering about in the dusk, and never had but one eye amongst us, and that one you have stolen away. Oh, give it back, good stranger!—whoever you are, give it back!"

All this while the Three Gray Women were groping with their outstretched hands, and trying their utmost to get hold of Perseus. But he took good care to keep out of their reach.

"My respectable dames!" said he,—for his mother had taught him to use always the greatest civility,—"I hold your eye fast in my hand, and shall keep it safely for you, until you please to tell me where to find these Nymphs. The Nymphs, I mean, who keep the enchanted wallet, the flying slippers, and the what is it?—the helmet of invisibility!"

"Mercy on us, sisters! what is the young man talking about?" exclaimed Scarecrow, Nightmare, and Shakejoint, one to another, with great appearance of astonishment. "A pair of flying slippers, quoth he! His heels would quickly fly higher than his head, if he were silly enough to put them on. And a helmet of invisibility! How could a helmet make him invisible, unless it were big enough for him to hide under it? And an enchanted wallet! What sort of a contrivance may that be, I wonder? No, no, good stranger! we can tell you nothing of these marvellous things. You have two eyes of your own, and we have but a single one amongst us three. You can find out such wonders better than three blind old creatures, like us."

Perseus, hearing them talk in this way, began really to think that the Gray Women knew nothing of the matter; and, as it grieved him to have put them to so much trouble, he was just on the point of restoring their eye, and asking pardon for his rudeness in snatching it away. But Quicksilver caught his hand.

"Don't let them make a fool of you!" said he. "These Three Gray Women are the only persons in the world that can tell you where to find the Nymphs; and, unless you get that information, you will never succeed in cutting off the head of Medusa with the snaky locks. Keep fast hold of the eye, and all will go well."

As it turned out, Quicksilver was in the right. There are but few things that people prize so much as they do their eyesight; and the Gray Women valued their single eye as highly as if it had been half a dozen, which was the number they ought to have had. Finding that there was no other way of recovering it, they at last told Perseus what he wanted to know. No sooner had they done so, than he immediately, and with the utmost respect, clapped the eye into the vacant socket in one of their foreheads, thanked them for their kindness, and bade them farewell. Before the young man was out of hearing, however, they had got into a new dispute, because he happened to have given the eye to Scarecrow, who had already taken her turn of it when their trouble with Perseus commenced.

It is greatly to be feared that the Three Gray Women were very much in the habit of disturbing their mutual harmony by bickerings of this sort; which was more the pity, as they could not conveniently do without one another, and were evidently intended to be inseparable companions. As a general rule, I would advise all people, whether sisters or brothers, old or young, who chance to have but one eye amongst them, to cultivate forbearance, and not all insist upon peeping through it at once.

Quicksilver and Perseus, in the meantime, were making the best of their way in quest of the Nymphs. The old dames had given them such particular directions, that they were not long in finding them out. They proved to be very different persons from Nightmare, Shakejoint, and Scarecrow; for, instead of being old, they were young and beautiful; and instead of one eye amongst the sisterhood, each Nymph had two exceedingly bright eyes of her own, with which she looked very kindly at Perseus. They seemed to be acquainted with Quicksilver; and, when he told them the adventure which Perseus had undertaken, they made no difficulty about giving him the valuable articles that were in their custody. In the first place, they brought out what appeared to be a small purse, made of deer skin, and curiously embroidered, and bade him be sure and keep it safe. This was the magic wallet. The Nymphs next produced a pair of shoes, or slippers, or sandals, with a nice little pair of wings at the heel of each.

"Put them on, Perseus," said Quicksilver. "You will

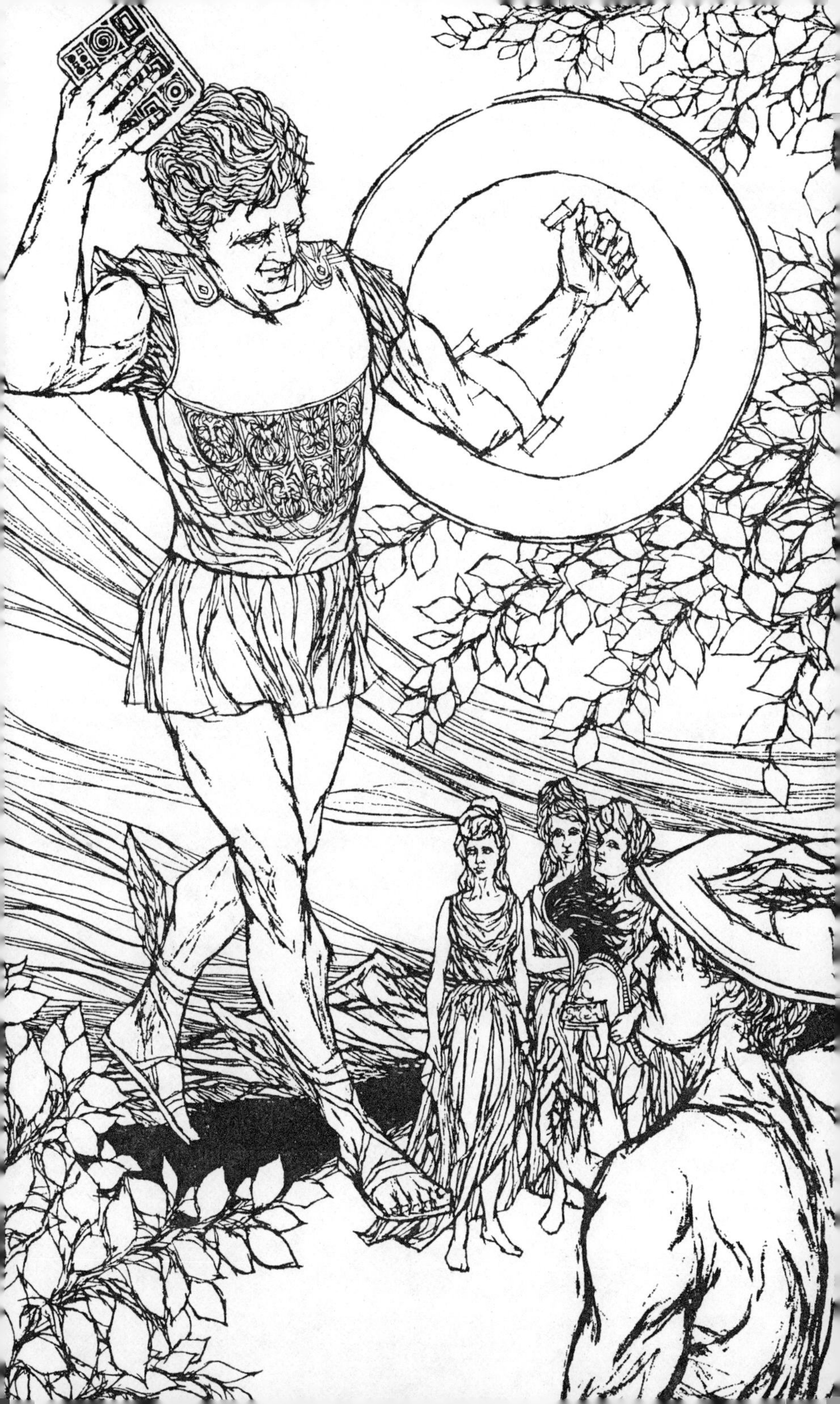

find yourself as light-heeled as you can desire for the remainder of our journey."

So Perseus proceeded to put one of the slippers on, while he laid the other on the ground by his side. Unexpectedly, however, this other slipper spread its wings, fluttered off the ground, and would probably have flown away, if Quicksilver had not made a leap, and luckily caught it in the air.

"Be more careful," said he, as he gave it back to Perseus. "It would frighten the birds up aloft, if they should see a flying slipper amongst them."

When Perseus had got on both of these wonderful slippers, he was altogether too buoyant to tread on earth. Making a step or two, lo and behold! upward he popped into the air, high above the heads of Quicksilver and the Nymphs, and found it very difficult to clamber down again. Winged slippers, and all such high-flying contrivances, are seldom quite easy to manage until one grows a little accustomed to them. Quicksilver laughed at his companion's involuntary activity, and told him that he must not be in so desperate a hurry, but must wait for the invisible helmet.

The good-natured Nymphs had the helmet, with its dark tuft of waving plumes, all in readiness to put upon his head. And now there happened about as wonderful an incident as anything that I have yet told you. The instant before the helmet was put on, there stood Perseus, a beautiful young man, with golden ringlets and rosy cheeks, the crooked sword by his side, and the brightly polished shield upon his arm,—a figure that seemed all made up of courage, sprightliness, and glorious light. But when the helmet had descended over his white brow, there was no longer any Perseus to be seen! Nothing but empty air! Even the helmet, that covered him with its invisibility, had vanished!

"Where are you, Perseus?" asked Quicksilver.

"Why, here, to be sure!" answered Perseus, very quietly, although his voice seemed to come out of the transparent atmosphere. "Just where I was a moment ago. Don't you see me?"

"No, indeed!" answered his friend. "You are hidden under the helmet. But, if I cannot see you, neither can the Gorgons. Follow me, therefore, and we will try your dexterity in using the winged slippers."

With these words, Quicksilver's cap spread its wings, as if his head were about to fly away from his shoulders; but his whole figure rose lightly into the air, and Perseus followed. By the time they had ascended a few hundred feet, the young man began to feel what a delightful thing it was to leave the dull earth so far beneath him, and to be able to flit about like a bird.

It was now deep night. Perseus looked upward, and saw the round, bright, silvery moon, and thought that he should desire nothing better than to soar up thither, and spend his life there. Then he looked downward again, and saw the earth, with its seas and lakes, and the silver courses of its rivers, and its snowy mountain peaks, and the breadth of its fields, and the dark cluster of its woods, and its cities of white marble; and, with the moonshine sleeping over the whole scene, it was as beautiful as the moon or any star could be. And, among other objects, he saw the island of Seriphus, where his dear mother was. Sometimes he and Quicksilver approached a cloud, that, at a distance, looked as if it were made of fleecy silver; although, when they plunged into it, they found themselves chilled and moistened with gray mist. So swift was their flight, however, that, in an instant, they emerged from the cloud into the moonlight again. Once, a high-soaring eagle flew right against the invisible Perseus. The bravest sights were the meteors, that gleamed suddenly out, as if a bonfire had been kindled in the sky, and made the moonshine pale for as much as a hundred miles around them.

As the two companions flew onward, Perseus fancied that he could hear the rustle of a garment close by his side; and it was on the side opposite to the one where he beheld Quicksilver, yet only Quicksilver was visible.

"Whose garment is this," inquired Perseus, "that keeps rustling close beside me in the breeze?"

"Oh, it is my sister's!" answered Quicksilver. "She is coming along with us, as I told you she would. We could do nothing without the help of my sister. You have no idea how wise she is. She has such eyes, too! Why, she can see you, at this moment, just as distinctly as if you were not invisible; and I'll venture to say, she will be the first to discover the Gorgons."

By this time, in their swift voyage through the air, they had come within sight of the great ocean, and were soon flying over it. Far beneath them, the waves tossed themselves tumultuously in mid-sea, or rolled a white surf-line upon the long beaches, or foamed against the rocky cliffs, with a roar that was thunderous, in the lower world; although it became a gentle murmur, like the voice of a baby half asleep, before it reached the ears of Perseus. Just then a voice spoke in the air close by him. It seemed to be a woman's voice, and was melodious, though not exactly what might be called sweet, but grave and mild.

"Perseus," said the voice, "there are the Gorgons."

"Where?" exclaimed Perseus. "I cannot see them."

"On the shore of that island beneath you," replied the voice. "A pebble, dropped from your hand, would strike in the midst of them."

"I told you she would be the first to discover them," said Quicksilver to Perseus. "And there they are!"

Straight downward, two or three thousand feet below him, Perseus perceived a small island, with the sea breaking into white foam all around its rocky shore, except on one side, where there was a beach of snowy sand. He descended towards it, and, looking earnestly at a cluster or heap of brightness, at the foot of a precipice of black rocks, behold, there were the terrible Gorgons! They lay fast asleep, soothed by the thunder of the sea; for it required a tumult that would have deafened everybody else to lull such fierce creatures into slumber. The moonlight glistened on their steely scales, and on their golden wings, which drooped idly over the sand. Their brazen claws, horrible to look at, were thrust out, and clutched the wave-beaten fragments of rock, while the sleeping Gorgons dreamed of tearing some poor mortal all to pieces. The snakes that served them instead of hair seemed likewise to be asleep; although, now and then, one would writhe, and lift its head, and thrust out its forked tongue, emitting a drowsy hiss, and then let itself subside among its sister snakes.

The Gorgons were more like an awful, gigantic kind of insect,—immense, golden-winged beetles, or dragon-flies, or things of that sort,—at once ugly and beautiful,—than like anything else; only that they were a thousand and a million times as big. And, with all this, there was something partly human about them, too. Luckily for Perseus, their faces were completely hidden from him by the posture in which they lay; for, had he but looked one instant at them, he would have fallen heavily out of the air, an image of senseless stone.

"Now," whispered Quicksilver, as he hovered by the side of Perseus,—"now is your time to do the deed! Be quick; for, if one of the Gorgons should awake, you are too late!"

"Which shall I strike at?" asked Perseus, drawing his sword and descending a little lower. "They all three look alike. All three have snaky locks. Which of the three is Medusa?"

It must be understood that Medusa was the only one of these dragon-monsters whose head Perseus could possibly cut off. As for the other two, let him have the sharpest sword that ever was forged, and he might have hacked away by the hour together, without doing them the least harm.

"Be cautious," said the calm voice which had before spoken to him. "One of the Gorgons is stirring in her sleep, and is just about to turn over. That is Medusa. Do not look at her! The sight would turn you to stone! Look at the reflection of her face and figure in the bright mirror of your shield."

Perseus now understood Quicksilver's motive for so earnestly exhorting him to polish his shield. In its surface he could safely look at the reflection of the Gorgon's face. And there it was,—that terrible countenance,—mirrored in the brightness of the shield, with the moonlight falling over it, and displaying all its horror. The snakes, whose venomous natures could not altogether sleep, kept twisting themselves over the forehead. It was the fiercest and most horrible face that ever was seen or imagined, and yet with a strange, fearful, and savage kind of beauty in it. The eyes were closed, and the Gorgon was still in a deep slumber; but there was an unquiet expression disturbing her features, as if the monster was troubled with an ugly dream. She gnashed her white tusks, and dug into the sand with her brazen claws.

The snakes, too, seemed to feel Medusa's dream, and to be made more restless by it. They twined themselves into tumultuous knots, writhed fiercely, and uplifted a hundred hissing heads, without opening their eyes.

"Now, now!" whispered Quicksilver, who was growing impatient. "Make a dash at the monster!"

"But be calm," said the grave, melodious voice, at the young man's side. "Look in your shield, as you fly downward, and take care that you do not miss your first stroke."

Perseus flew cautiously downward, still keeping his eyes on Medusa's face, as reflected in his shield. The nearer he came, the more terrible did the snaky visage and metallic body of the monster grow. At last, when he found himself hovering over her within arm's length, Perseus uplifted his sword, while at the same instant, each separate snake upon the Gorgon's head stretched threateningly upward, and Medusa unclosed her eyes. But she awoke too late. The sword was sharp; the stroke fell like a lightning-flash; and the head of the wicked Medusa tumbled from her body.

"Admirably done!" cried Quicksilver. "Make haste, and clap the head into your magic wallet."

To the astonishment of Perseus, the small, embroidered wallet, which he had hung about his neck, and which had hitherto been no bigger than a purse, grew all at once large enough to contain Medusa's head. As quick as thought, he snatched it up, with the snakes still writhing upon it, and thrust it in.

"Your task is done," said the calm voice. "Now fly; for the other Gorgons will do their utmost to take vengeance for Medusa's death."

It was, indeed, necessary to take flight; for Perseus had not done the deed so quietly but that the clash of his sword, and the hissing of the snakes, and the thump of Medusa's head as it tumbled upon the sea-beaten sand, awoke the other two monsters. There they sat, for an instant, sleepily rubbing their eyes with their brazen fingers, while all the snakes on their heads reared themselves on end with surprise, and with venomous malice against they knew not what. But when the Gorgons saw the scaly carcass of Medusa, headless, and her golden wings all ruffled, and half spread out on the sand, it was really awful to hear what yells and screeches they set up. And then the snakes! They sent forth a hundred-fold hiss, with one consent, and Medusa's snakes answered them out of the magic wallet.

No sooner were the Gorgons broad awake than they

hurtled upward into the air, brandishing their brass talons, gnashing their horrible tusks, and flapping their huge wings so wildly, that some of the golden feathers were shaken out, and floated down upon the shore. And there, perhaps, those very feathers lie scattered, till this day. Up rose the Gorgons, as I tell you, staring horribly about, in hopes of turning somebody to stone. Had Perseus looked them in the face, or had he fallen into their clutches, his poor mother would never have kissed her boy again! But he took good care to turn his eyes another way; and, as he wore the helmet of invisibility, the Gorgons knew not in what direction to follow him; nor did he fail to make the best use of the winged slippers, by soaring upward a perpendicular mile or so. At that height, when the screams of those abominable creatures sounded faintly beneath him, he made a straight course for the island of Seriphus, in order to carry Medusa's head to King Polydectes.

I have no time to tell you of several marvelous things that befell Perseus, on his way homeward; such as his killing a hideous sea-monster, just as it was on the point of devouring a beautiful maiden; nor how he changed an enormous giant into a mountain of stone, merely by showing him the head of the Gorgon. If you doubt this latter story, you may make a voyage to Africa, some day or other, and see the very mountain, which is still known by the ancient giant's name.

Finally our brave Perseus arrived at the island, where he expected to see his dear mother. But, during his absence, the wicked king had treated Danaë so very ill that she was compelled to make her escape, and had taken refuge in a temple, where some good old priests were extremely kind to her. These praiseworthy priests, and the kind-hearted fisherman, who had first shown hospitality to Danaë and little Perseus when he found them afloat in the chest, seem to have been the only persons on the island who cared about doing right. All the rest of the people, as well as King Polydectes himself, were remarkably ill-behaved, and deserved no better destiny than that which was now to happen.

Not finding his mother at home, Perseus went straight to the palace, and was immediately ushered into the presence of the King. Polydectes was by no means rejoiced to see him; for he had felt almost certain in his own evil mind, that the Gorgons would have torn the poor young man to pieces, and have eaten him up, out of the way. However, seeing him safely returned, he put the best face he could upon the matter and asked Perseus how he had succeeded.

"Have you performed your promise?" inquired he. "Have you brought me the head of Medusa with the snaky locks? If not, young man, it will cost you dear; for I must have a bridal present for the beautiful Princess Hippodamia, and there is nothing else that she would admire so much."

"Yes, please your Majesty," answered Perseus, in a quiet way, as if it were no very wonderful deed for such a young man as he to perform. "I have brought you the Gorgon's head, snaky locks and all!"

"Indeed! Pray let me see it," quoth King Polydectes. "It must be a very curious spectacle, if all that travellers tell about it be true!"

"Your Majesty is in the right," replied Perseus. "It is really an object that will be pretty certain to fix the regards of all who look at it. And, if your Majesty think fit, I would suggest that a holiday be proclaimed, and that all your Majesty's subjects be summoned to behold this wonderful curiosity. Few of them, I imagine, have seen a Gorgon's head before, and perhaps never may again!"

The king well knew that his subjects were an idle set of reprobates, and very fond of sight-seeing, as idle persons usually are. So he took the young man's advice, and sent out heralds and messengers, in all directions, to blow the trumpet at the street corners, and in the marketplaces, and wherever two roads met, and summon everybody to court. Thither, accordingly, came a great multitude of good-for-nothing vagabonds, all of whom, out of pure love of mischief, would have been glad if Perseus had met with some ill-hap in his encounter with the Gorgons. If there were any better people in the island (as I really hope there may have been, although the story tells nothing about any such), they stayed quietly at home, minding their business, and taking care of their little children. Most of the inhabitants, at all events, ran as fast as they could to the palace, and shoved, and pushed, and elbowed one another, in their eagerness to get near a balcony, on which Perseus showed himself, holding the embroidered wallet in his hand.

On a platform, within full view of the balcony, sat the mighty King Polydectes, amid his evil counsellors, and with his flattering courtiers in a semicircle round about him. Monarch, counsellors, courtiers, and subjects, all gazed eagerly towards Perseus.

"Show us the head! Show us the head!" shouted the people; and there was a fierceness in their cry as if they would tear Perseus to pieces, unless he should satisfy them with what he had to show. "Show us the head of Medusa with the snaky locks!"

A feeling of sorrow and pity came over the youthful Perseus.

"O King Polydectes," cried he, "and ye many people, I am very loath to show you the Gorgon's head!"

"Ah, the villain and coward!" yelled the people more fiercely than before. "He is making game of us! He has no Gorgon's head! Show us the head, if you have it, or we will take your own head for a football!"

The evil counsellors whispered bad advice in the king's ear; the courtiers murmured, with one consent, that Perseus had shown disrespect to their royal lord and master; and the great King Polydectes himself waved his hand, and ordered him, with the stern, deep voice of authority, on his peril, to produce the head.

"Show me the Gorgon's head, or I will cut off your own!"

And Perseus sighed.

"This instant," repeated Polydectes, "or you die!"

"Behold it, then!" cried Perseus, in a voice like the blast of a trumpet.

And suddenly, holding up the head, not an eyelid had time to wink before the wicked King Polydectes, his evil counsellors, and all his fierce subjects were no longer anything but the mere images of a monarch and his people. They were all fixed forever, in the look and attitude of that moment! At the first glimpse of the terrible head of Medusa, they whitened into marble! And Perseus thrust the head back into his wallet, and went to tell his dear mother that she need no longer be afraid of the wicked King Polydectes.

TALKING ABOUT THE STORY

1. Some of the characters in this story used trickery to attain their goals.
    Polydectes thought he would get rid of Perseus. Why? How?
    How did Perseus trick the Gray Women? Why?
    What made it possible for Perseus to behead Medusa without looking at her? Did you guess Quicksilver's plan? When?
2. "'... Perhaps you may have heard of me. I have more names than one; but the name of Quicksilver suits me as well as any other....'" Did any clues help you guess Quicksilver's other names? Who was his sister?
    What assistance did Quicksilver give Perseus? Did the hero ever act without advice from Quicksilver?
3. Sometimes situations do not turn out as people plan. Polydectes' scheme to kill Perseus backfired. How?
4. The number *three* occurs quite often in mythology. What gifts did Perseus receive from the Nymphs? Can you think of other "triple" objects or people from "Perseus"? from other stories you've read?

WORDS FROM MYTHOLOGY

Mercury

Have you ever broken a thermometer? What did the mercury look like? What happened when you tried to pick it up? Why do you suppose Mercury is sometimes called Quicksilver? How would a person with a *mercurial* temperament act?

GREEK WORDS IN OUR LANGUAGE

Here are some Greek word parts. Do you know their meanings?

micro (small)	*psych* (mind)
auto (self)	*graphy* (writing)
bio (life)	*phone* (sound)
demos (people)	*cracy* (people)
tele (far)	*logy* (science)

The parts *tele* and *phone* combine to form *telephone*—the voice from far away. *Auto* combines with *graph(y)* to form *autograph*—self-writing, or a signature.

How many other English words can you make up by combining the word parts?

Is the story of Perseus *biographical* or *autobiographical*? Was the kingdom of Polydectes an *autocracy* or a *democracy*?

IDEAS FOR WRITING

Imagine that you were one of the Three Gray Women—Nightmare, Scarecrow, or Shakejoint—and Perseus stole your eye. What did you do while Perseus talked? Did you try to snatch the eye away from him? Did you know where he stood? Describe your thoughts, comments, and actions.

Odysseus was a Greek hero of the Trojan War, the ten-year struggle between Greece and Troy. For ten years after the war the gods buffeted him from land to land, delaying his return home to Ithaca. During his wanderings, he and his men visited King Alcinous's court, where Odysseus told about some of their harrowing experiences.

BY PADRAIC COLUM

odysseus and polyphemus

'I am Odysseus,* son of Laertes,* and my land is Ithaka, an island around which many islands lie. Ithaka is a rugged isle, but a good nurse of hardy men, and I, for one, have found that there is no place fairer than a man's own land. But now I will tell thee, King, and tell the Princes and Captains and Councillors of the Phaeacians,* the tale of my wanderings.'

'The wind bore my ships from the coast of Troy, and with our white sails hoisted we came to the cape that is called Malea.* Now if we had been able to double this cape we should soon have come to our own country, all unhurt. But the north wind came and swept us from our course and drove us wandering past Cythera.'

'Then for nine days we were borne onward by terrible winds, and away from all known

*Odysseus (ō-dis′-ūs)   *Phaeacians (fē′-āshənz)
*Laertes (lā-ūr′-tēz)   *Malea (mə-lē′-ə)

lands. On the tenth day we came to a strange country. Many of my men landed there. The people of that land were harmless and friendly, but the land itself was most dangerous. For there grew there the honey-sweet fruit of the lotus that makes all men forgetful of their past and neglectful of their future. And those of my men who ate the lotus that the dwellers of that land offered them became forgetful of their country and of the way before them. They wanted to abide forever in the land of the lotus. They wept when they thought of all the toils before them and of all they had endured. I commanded those who had ate of the lotus to go at once aboard the ships. I led them back to the ships, and I had to place them beneath the benches and leave them in bonds. Then, when I had got all my men upon the ships, we made haste to sail away.'

'Later we came to the land of the Cyclôpes,* a giant people. There is a waste island outside the harbour of their land, and on it there is a well of bright water that has poplars growing round it. We came to that empty island, and we beached our ships and took down our sails.'

'As soon as the dawn came we went through the empty island, starting the wild goats that were there in flocks, and shooting them with our arrows. We killed so many wild goats there that we had nine for each ship. Afterwards we looked across to the land of the Cyclôpes, and we heard the sound of voices and saw the smoke of fires and heard the bleating of flocks of sheep and goats.'

'I called my companions together and I said, "It would be well for some of us to go to that other island. With

*Cyclôpes (sī'-klō-pēz)

my own ship and with the company that is on it I shall go there. The rest of you abide here. I will find out what manner of men live there, and whether they will treat us kindly and give us gifts that are due to strangers—gifts of provisions for our voyage." '

'We embarked and we came to the land. There was a cave near the sea, and round the cave there were mighty flocks of sheep and goats. I took twelve men with me and I left the rest to guard the ship. We went into the cave and found no man there. There were baskets filled with cheeses, and vessels of whey, and pails and bowls of milk. My men wanted me to take some of the cheeses and drive off some of the lambs and kids and come away. But this I would not do, for I would rather that he who owned the stores would give us of his own free will the offerings that were due to strangers.'

'While we were in the cave, he whose dwelling it was, returned to it. He carried on his shoulder a great pile of wood for his fire. Never in our lives did we see a creature so frightful as this Cyclops* was. He was a giant in size, and, what made him terrible to behold, he had but one eye, and that single eye was in his forehead. He cast down on the ground the pile of wood that he carried, making such a din that we fled in terror into the corners and recesses of the cave. Next he drove his flocks into the cave and began to milk his ewes and goats. And when he had the flocks within, he took up a stone that not all of our strengths could move and set it as a door to the mouth of the cave.'

'The Cyclops kindled his fire, and when it blazed up he saw us in the corners and recesses. He spoke to us. We

*Cyclops (sī'-klops)

knew not what he said, but our hearts were shaken with terror at the sound of his deep voice.'

'I spoke to him saying that we were Greeks on our way home from the taking of Troy, and I begged him to deal with us kindly, for the sake of Zeus who is ever in the company of strangers and suppliants. But he answered me saying, "We Cyclôpes pay no heed to Zeus, nor to any of thy gods. In our strength and our power we deem that we are mightier than they. I will not spare thee, neither will I give thee aught for the sake of Zeus, but only as my own spirit bids me. And first I would have thee tell me how you came to our land." '

'I knew it would be better not to let the Cyclops know that my ship and my companions were at the harbour of the island. Therefore I spoke to him guilefully, telling him that my ship had been broken on the rocks, and that I and the men with me were the only ones who had escaped utter doom.'

'I begged again that he would deal with us as just men deal with strangers and suppliants, but he, without saying a word, laid hands upon two of my men, and swinging them by the legs, dashed their brains out on the earth. He cut them to pieces and ate them before our very eyes. We wept and we prayed to Zeus as we witnessed a deed so terrible.'

'Next the Cyclops stretched himself amongst his sheep and went to sleep beside the fire. Then I debated whether I should take my sharp sword in my hand, and feeling where his heart was, stab him there. But second thoughts held me back from doing this. I might be able to kill him as he slept, but not even with my companions could I roll away the great stone that closed the mouth of the cave.'

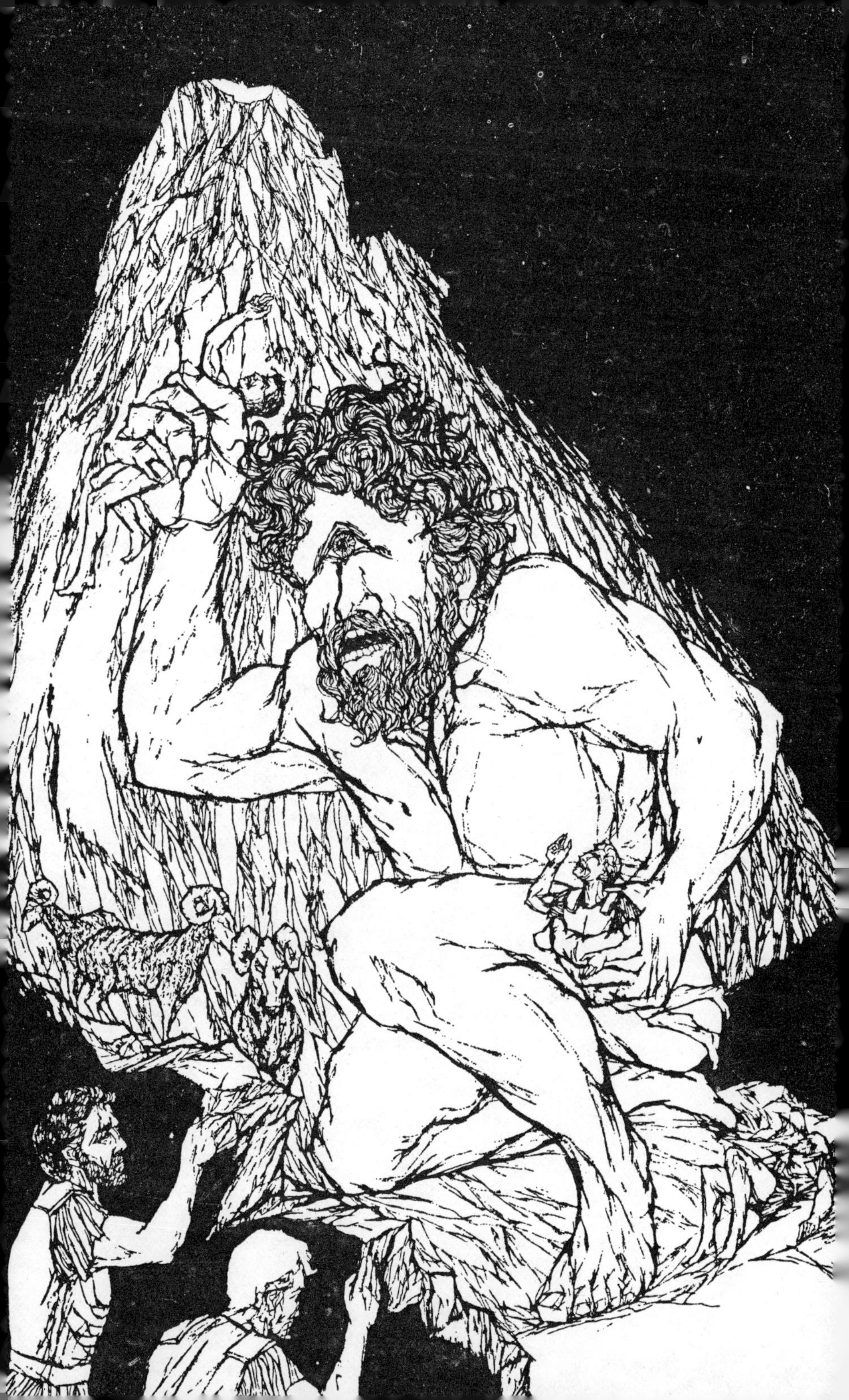

'Dawn came, and the Cyclops awakened, kindled his fire and milked his flocks. Then he seized two others of my men and made ready for his mid-day meal. And now he rolled away the great stone and drove his flocks out of the cave.'

'I had pondered on a way of escape, and I had thought of something that might be done to baffle the Cyclops. I had with me a great skin of sweet wine, and I thought that if I could make him drunken with wine I and my companions might be able for him. But there were other preparations to be made first. On the floor of the cave there was a great beam of olive wood which the Cyclops had cut to make a club when the wood should be seasoned. It was yet green. I and my companions went and cut off a fathom's length of the wood, and sharpened it to a point and took it to the fire and hardened it in the glow. Then I hid the beam in a recess of the cave.'

'The Cyclops came back in the evening, and opening up the cave drove in his flocks. Then he closed the cave again with the stone and went and milked his ewes and his goats. Again he seized two of my companions. I went to the terrible creature with a bowl of wine in my hands. He took it and drank it and cried out, "Give me another bowl of this, and tell me thy name that I may give thee gifts for bringing me this honey-tasting drink."'

'Again I spoke to him guilefully and said, "Noman is my name. Noman my father and my mother call me."'

'"Give me more of the drink, Noman," he shouted. "And the gift that I shall give to thee is that I shall make thee the last of thy fellows to be eaten."'

'I gave him wine again, and when he had taken the third bowl he sank backwards with his face upturned, and sleep came upon him. Then I, with four companions, took that beam of olive wood, now made into a hard and pointed stake, and thrust it into the ashes of the fire. When the pointed end began to glow we drew it out of the flame. Then I and my companions laid hold on the great stake and, dashing at the Cyclops, thrust it into his eye. He raised a terrible cry that made the rocks ring and we dashed away into the recesses of the cave.'

'His cries brought other Cyclôpes to the mouth of the cave, and they, naming him as Polyphemus,* called out and asked him what ailed him to cry. "Noman," he shrieked out, "Noman is slaying me by guile." They answered him saying, "If no man is slaying thee, there is nothing we can do for thee, Polyphemus. What ails thee has been sent to thee by the gods." Saying this, they went away from the mouth of the cave without attempting to move away the stone.'

'Polyphemus then, groaning with pain, rolled away the stone and sat before the mouth of the cave with his hands outstretched, thinking that he would catch us as we dashed out. I showed my companions how we might pass by him. I laid hands on certain rams of the flock and I lashed three of them together with supple rods. Then on the middle ram I put a man of my company. Thus every three rams carried a man. As soon as the dawn had come the rams hastened out to the pasture, and, as they passed, Polyphemus laid hands on the first and the third of each three that went by. They passed out and Polyphemus did not guess that a ram that he did not touch carried out a man.'

'For myself, I took a ram that was the strongest and fleeciest of the whole flock and I placed myself under

*Polyphemus (pol'-i-fē'-məs)

him, clinging to the wool of his belly. As this ram, the best of all his flock, went by, Polyphemus, laying his hands upon him, said, "Would that you, the best of my flock, were endowed with speech, so that you might tell me where Noman, who has blinded me, has hidden himself." The ram went by him, and when he had gone a little way from the cave I loosed myself from him and went and set my companions free.'

'We gathered together many of Polyphemus' sheep and we drove them down to our ship. The men we had left behind would have wept when they heard what had happened to six of their companions. But I bade them take on board the sheep we had brought and pull the ship away from that land. Then when we had drawn a certain distance from the shore I could not forbear to shout my taunts into the cave of Polyphemus.

' "Cyclops," I cried, "you thought that you had the company of a fool and a weakling to eat. But you have been worsted by me, and your evil deeds have been punished." '

'So I shouted, and Polyphemus came to the mouth of the cave with great anger in his heart. He took up rocks and cast them at the ship and they fell before the prow. The men bent to the oars and pulled the ship away or it would have been broken by the rocks he cast. And when we were further away I shouted to him:

' "Cyclops, if any man should ask who it was set his mark upon you, say that he was Odysseus, the son of Laertes." '

'Then I heard Polyphemus cry out, "I call upon Poseidon, the god of the sea, whose son I am, to avenge me upon you, Odysseus. I call upon Poseidon to grant that you, Odysseus, may never come to your home, or if the gods have ordained your return, that you come to it after much toil and suffering, in an evil plight and in a stranger's ship, to find sorrow in your home." '

'So Polyphemus prayed, and, to my evil fortune, Poseidon heard his prayer. But we went on in our ship rejoicing at our escape. We came to the waste island where my other ships were. All the company rejoiced to see us, although they had to mourn for their six companions slain by Polyphemus. We divided amongst the ships the sheep we had taken from Polyphemus' flock and we sacrificed to the gods. At the dawn of the next day we raised the sails on each ship and we sailed away.'

TALKING ABOUT THE STORY

1. Odysseus and Polyphemus were as different in temperament as they were in appearance. Which of the following words describe the Greek warrior? the giant? Why?

Strong	Cruel	Wise	Thoughtful
Cunning	Brave	Gluttonous	Temperamental

2. Jason, Theseus, Hercules, and Perseus depended on strength or help from outside sources for their success. Did Odysseus? How did Odysseus outwit Polyphemus?

3. Did Odysseus' actions and words give you any hints about the treatment of strangers in those days?

EXPRESSIONS FROM MYTHOLOGY

What effect did the lotus have on people who ate it? If you heard that someone had passed his life as a "lotus-eater," what would that mean?

WORDS FROM MYTHOLOGY

Odyssey

Odysseus wandered for ten years after the Trojan War. From knowing this fact, can you guess what an *odyssey* is? There is a book entitled *An American Doctor's Odyssey*. Can you guess its contents?

IDEAS FOR WRITING

1. Suppose that Hercules was trapped in Polyphemus' cave. How would he escape? Would he use his bare hands? his bow and arrows? assistance from an Olympian? What would Jason do if he were trapped there? Theseus? Perseus? Substitute another hero in Odysseus' place. Describe his escape from the Cyclops.
2. Odysseus might have outwitted a different monster on another adventure. What kind of monster? part man, part plant? a mountain that came to life? How would the monster terrify its victims? Create a monster and write about Odysseus' encounter with it.

section 3

tales of the trojan war

THE EPIC struggle of the ancient world was the Trojan War, a ten-year conflict between Greece and Troy. About one thousand B.C., Homer, the first writer to record the myths and legends of Greece, told the story of that conflict in his poem, *The Iliad*.

For a long time, people accepted Homer's tale as historical truth. But then scholars began to wonder if Troy had ever really existed. In 1870 Heinrich Schliemann, an amateur German archaeologist, excavated a mound near the Aegean Sea in Asia Minor. His findings led to the discovery of the sixteen-foot-thick walls which had surrounded and fortified the ancient city of Troy. Scholars now know that Troy, established as a small stronghold about three thousand B.C., underwent at least nine destructions and rebuildings. Homer's *Iliad*, which immortalized Troy as one of the most famous cities the world has ever known, is based on battles that probably occurred in the early twelfth century B.C.

The story of the Trojan War has enthralled people for centuries. It tells how three goddesses argued over which one was the most beautiful; how their argument led to the elopement of the Trojan prince Paris with Queen Helen of Sparta, Greece; and how the kings and warriors of Greece sailed to Troy to rescue Helen.

The three war stories you will read are retold by Robert Graves. They tell how the war began and how it ended, as well as something of the titantic ten-year struggle itself.

Prophecies of doom surrounding a baby's birth... King Priam of Troy, annoyed with his sister Hesione for not returning to Troy from Salamis, Greece... a beauty contest among three goddesses... the elopement of Queen Helen of Sparta, Greece. Read how these events triggered one of the most memorable seiges in history— the Trojan War.

BY ROBERT GRAVES

paris and queen helen

Here is the story of Paris and Helen. Paris was Priam's* son by Queen Hecuba* who, just before his birth, dreamed that instead of a child she bore a blazing faggot, from which wriggled countless fiery serpents. Priam asked Apollo's prophet Calchas* what the dream meant. Calchas answered: 'This child will be Troy's ruin. Cut his throat as soon as he is born!' Priam could not bring himself to kill any baby, especially his own son, but the warning frightened him; so he gave the child to his chief cattleman, saying: 'Leave him behind a bush somewhere in the woods on Mount Ida, and don't go there again for nine days.'

The cattleman obeyed. But on the ninth day, passing through the bushy valley in which Paris had been left, he found a she-bear suckling him. Amazed at this sight, the cattleman brought Paris up with his own children.

*Priam (prī'-am) *Calchas (kal'-kəs)
*Hecuba (hek'-yoo-bə)

209

Paris grew to be tall, handsome, strong and clever. He was always invited by the other cattlemen to judge bullfights. Almighty Zeus, watching from his palace on far-off Olympus, noticed how honestly he gave his verdict on such occasions; and one day chose him to preside over a beauty contest at which he did not care to appear himself. This is what had happened. The Goddess of Quarrels, Eris* by name, was not invited to a famous wedding attended by all the other gods and goddesses. Eris spitefully threw a golden apple among the guests, after scratching on the peel: 'For the Most Beautiful!' They would have handed the apple to Thetis, as the bride; but were afraid of offending the three far more important goddesses present: Hera, Almighty Zeus's wife; Athene, his unmarried daughter, who was Goddess not only of Wisdom but of Battle; and his daughter-in-law Aphrodite, Goddess of Love. Each of them thought herself the most beautiful, and they began quarreling about the apple, as Eris had intended. Zeus's one hope of domestic peace lay in ordering a beauty contest and choosing an honest judge.

So Hermes, Herald of the Gods, flew down with the golden apple and a message for Paris from Zeus. 'Three goddesses,' he announced, 'will visit you here on Mount Ida, and Almighty Zeus's orders are that you shall award this apple to the most beautiful. They will all, of course, abide by your decision.' Paris disliked the task, but could not avoid it.

The goddesses arrived together, each in turn unveiling her beauty; and each in turn offering a bribe. Hera undertook to make Paris Emperor of Asia. Athene

*Eris (ē'-ris)

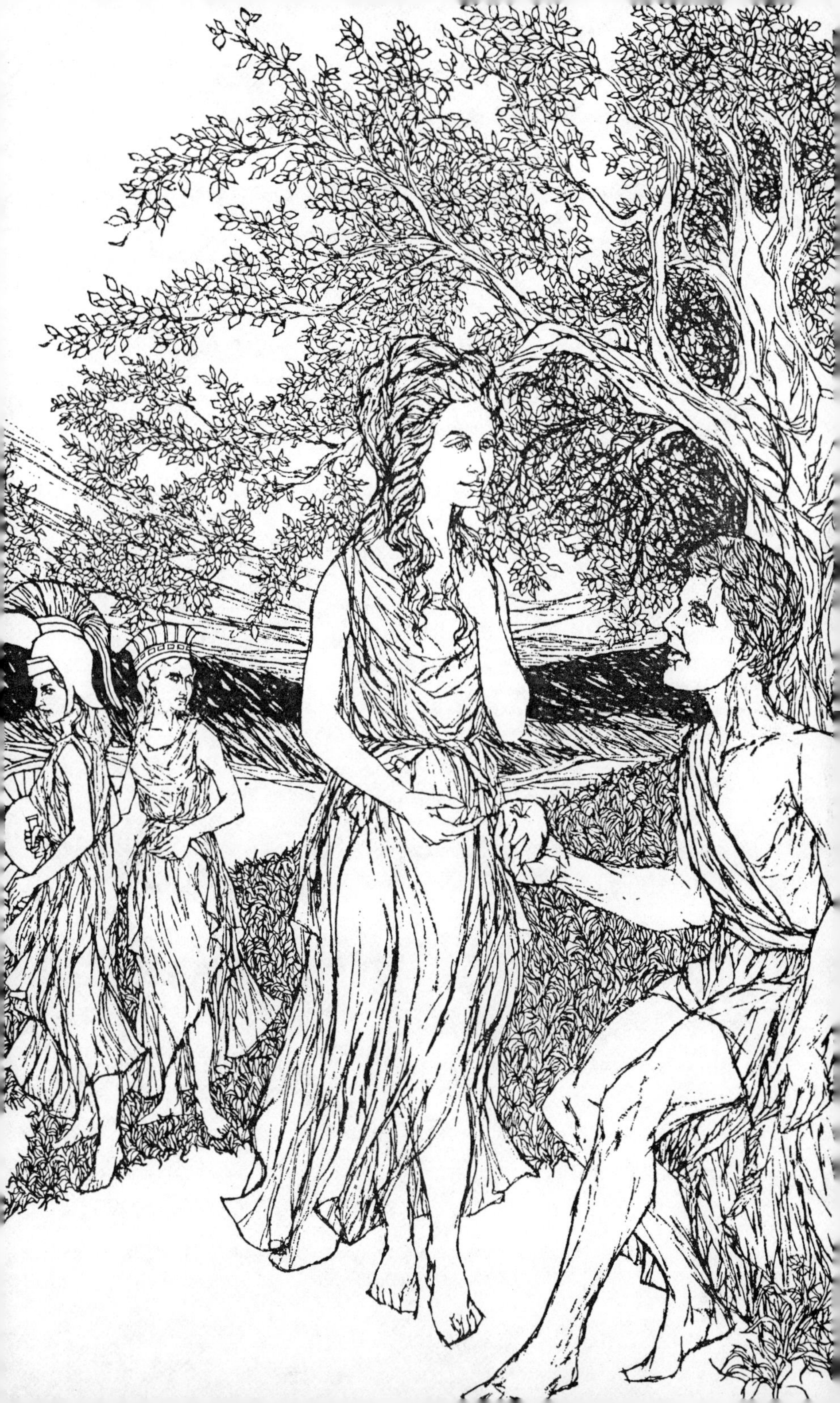

undertook to make him the wisest man alive and victorious in all his battles. But Aphrodite sidled up, saying: 'Darling Paris, I declare that you're the handsomest young fellow I've seen for years! Why waste your time here among bulls and cows and stupid cattlemen? Why not move to some rich city and lead a more interesting life? You deserve to marry a woman almost as beautiful as myself—let me suggest Queen Helen of Sparta. One look at you, and I'll make her fall so deep in love that she won't mind leaving her husband, her palace, her family—everything, for your sake!' Excited by Aphrodite's account of Helen's beauty, Paris handed her the apple; whereupon Hera and Athene went off angrily, arm in arm, to plot the destruction of the whole Trojan race.

Next day, Paris paid his first visit to Troy, and found an athletic festival in progress. His foster-father, the cattleman, who had come too, advised him against entering the boxing contest which was staged in front of Priam's throne; but Paris stepped forward and won the crown of victory by sheer courage rather than skill. He put his name down for the foot-race, too, and ran first. When Priam's sons challenged him to a longer race, he beat them again. They grew so annoyed, to think that a mere peasant had carried off three crowns of victory in a row, that they drew their swords. Paris ran for protection to the altar of Zeus, while his foster-father fell on his knees before Priam, crying: 'Your Majesty, pardon me! This is your lost son.'

The King summoned Hecuba, and Paris's foster-father showed her a rattle left in his hands when he was a baby.

She knew it at once; so they took Paris with them to the palace and there celebrated a huge banquet in honour of his return. Nevertheless, Calchas and the other priests of Apollo warned Priam that unless Paris were immediately put to death, Troy would go up in smoke. He answered: 'Better that Troy should burn, than that my wonderful son should die!'

Priam made ready a fleet to sail for Salamis and rescue his sister Queen Hesione,* by force of arms. Paris offered to take command, adding: 'And if we can't bring my aunt home, perhaps I may capture some Greek princess whom we can hold as a hostage.' He was of course already planning to carry off Helen, and had no intention of fetching back his old aunt, in whom no Trojan but Priam took the least interest, and who felt perfectly happy at Salamis.

While Priam was deciding whether he should give Paris the command, Menelaus,* King of Sparta, happened to visit Troy on some business matter. He made friends with Paris and invited him to Sparta; which enabled Paris to carry out his plan easily, using no more than a single fast ship. He and Menelaus sailed as soon as the wind blew favourably and, on arrival at Sparta, feasted together nine days running. Under Aphrodite's spell, Helen loved Paris at first sight, but was greatly embarrassed by his bold behaviour. He even dared to write 'I love Helen!' in wine spilt on the top of the banqueting table. Yet Menelaus, grieved by news of his father's death in Crete, noticed nothing; and when the nine days ended, he set sail for the funeral, leaving Helen to rule in his absence. This was no more than

*Hesione (he-sī'-a-ni)   *Menelaus (men'-ə-lā'-əs)

Helen's due, since he had become King of Sparta by marrying her.

That same night Helen and Paris eloped in his fast ship, putting aboard most of the palace treasures that she had inherited from her foster-father. And Paris stole a great mass of gold out of Apollo's temple, in revenge for the prophecy made by his priests that he should be killed at birth. Hera spitefully raised a heavy storm, which blew their ship to Cyprus; and Paris decided to stay there some months before he went home—Menelaus might be anchored off Troy, waiting to catch him. In Cyprus, where Paris had friends, he collected a fleet to raid Sidon,* a rich city on the coast of Palestine. The raid was a great success: Paris killed the Sidonian king, and captured vast quantities of treasure.

When at last he returned to Troy, his ship loaded with silver, gold and precious stones, the Trojans welcomed him rapturously. Everyone thought Helen so beautiful, beyond all comparison, that King Priam himself swore never to give her up, even in exchange for his sister Hesione, who was still held captive in Salamis. Paris quieted his enemies, the Trojan priests of Apollo, by handing them the gold robbed from the God's treasury at Sparta; and almost the only two people who took a gloomy view of what would now happen were Paris's sister Cassandra,* and her twin-brother Helenus,* both of whom possessed the gift of prophecy. This they had won accidentally, while still children, by falling asleep in Apollo's temple. The sacred serpents had come up and licked their ears, which enabled them to hear the God's secret voice. Yet it did them no good: because Apollo

*Sidon (sī'-d'n)   *Helenus (hel'-ə-nus)
*Cassandra (kə-san'-drə)

arranged that no one would believe their prophecies. Time after time Cassandra and Helenus had warned Priam never to let Paris visit Greece. Now they warned him to send Helen and her treasure back at once if he wanted to avoid a long and terrible war. Priam paid not the least attention.

TALKING ABOUT THE STORY

1. Predictions of disaster are common in Greek mythology. How did Priam and Hecuba attempt to avoid the disaster prophesied before the birth of Paris? How did their action lead to Paris's involvement with Zeus and the goddesses?

2. Three goddesses tried to influence Paris with bribes. What did Hera offer Paris? What did Athene? Aphrodite? How did the bribe of each goddess reflect her interests and attributes?

3. Sometimes people are not what they seem to be. Zeus thought Paris would be an honest judge. Why? Were you disappointed in Paris? Did Paris's behavior after the contest show he was a man of integrity? Explain.

4. Why was Queen Helen of Sparta important in the story? What part did her husband, King Menelaus, play in the story?

5. Which prophets and gods foretold doom in this story? What did each one say?

6. How would you summarize the events which led to the beginning of the Trojan War?

EXPRESSIONS FROM MYTHOLOGY

A point of disagreement today could be called an "apple of discord." Why?

GREEK WORDS IN OUR LANGUAGE

Archaeo is a Greek word that means "ancient." *Archaeology* is the study of ancient life by excavation. The *archaeopteryx*, a reptile-like bird, is now extinct.

Something especially old is *archaic*. For example, a shield unearthed at the site of Troy would be an *archaic* object. Try to think of other *archaic* items.

IDEAS FOR WRITING

Three gods are squabbling over an apple inscribed "For the Bravest." Zeus chooses you to settle the dispute. Which gods are involved? What are their bribes? Write about the bravery contest. Tell how you decide upon the winner.

INTERLUDE

When Hera learned that Paris and Helen had eloped, she sent her messenger, Iris, to tell Menelaus. Menelaus quickly summoned all of Helen's former suitors. These men assembled in accordance with a pledge they had made before Helen's betrothal —a pledge to assist Helen's future husband if the marriage should ever be challenged. After two years of preparation, the kings and warriors of Greece, under the leadership of Menelaus' brother Agamemnon, launched a thousand ships against Troy. The mightiest Greek chieftain in this expedition was Achilles, who was invulnerable except for one spot on his heel.

When Agamemnon and his men landed on the coast of Troy, they pulled their ships up on the beach, and erected a barricade of logs around them. This formed a camp facing the wall of Troy.

The Greeks had great strength; but so did the Trojans, led by Priam and his courageous son Hector, who was fated to meet Achilles in a struggle for his life.

The siege of Troy began. The gods took sides and alternated the advantage between the Greeks and the Trojans. Aphrodite naturally supported Paris and the other Trojans. So did Ares, Artemis, and Apollo; even Zeus assisted the Trojans at times. Hera and Athene, still resentful of the judgment of Paris, championed the Greek cause. Poseidon, Hermes, and Hephaestus also sided with the Greeks. The war continued for over nine years, before it culminated in a devastating series of events.

On the opposite page you can see who fought on each side in the war.

MAJOR ADVERSARIES IN THE TROJAN WAR

TROY		GREECE	
Priam	*King of Troy*	Menelaus	*King of Sparta*
Hecuba	*Queen of Troy*	Agamemnon	*Greek Warriors*
Paris	*Sons of Priam and Hecuba*	Odysseus	
Hector		Achilles	
Polydorus		Patroclus	
Deiphobus		Ajax	
Antenor	*Trojan Warriors*	Little Ajax	
Aeneas		Diomedes	
		Nestor	
Helen of Troy	*Formerly Queen of Sparta, Greece*	Sinon	
		Calchas	*Apollo's Prophet*
Andromache	*Hector's wife*		
Cassandra	*Twin daughter and son of Priam and Hecuba*		
Helenus			
Aphrodite	*Goddess of Love and Beauty*	Hera	*Queen of the Gods*
Ares	*God of War*	Athene	*Goddess of Wisdom*
Artemis	*Goddess of the Hunt*	Poseidon	*God of the Sea*
Apollo	*God of the Sun*	Hermes	*Messenger of the Gods*
Zeus	*King of the Gods*	Hephaestus	*God of the Forge*
Leto	*Mother of Apollo and Artemis*	Thetis	*Mother of Achilles*
Scamander	*A River God*		

The Greeks were suffering. Hector, with Zeus's aid, had driven them almost back to their ships. In addition, there was dissension among the Greeks. Achilles, furious because Agamemnon had demanded his slave-girl Briseis, retired to his tent and refused to fight, predicting a time when the Greeks would beg him to do so.

That time had come. Neither Agamemnon's bribes nor the pleadings of Achilles's friend Patroclus persuaded Achilles to join the battle.

Achilles Avenges Patroclus

BY ROBERT GRAVES

Patroclus* begged Achilles* to lend him his own suit of armour and the command of his warlike Myrmidons.* 'With their help,' he pleaded, 'I can drive away the Trojans before the fleet is burned and our surviving friends are massacred.' Achilles consented, but made Patroclus promise that once the camp had been cleared of enemies, he would not try to win further glory by chasing them back and attacking Troy itself.

Great Ajax* could no longer defend his ship, because Hector* lopped off the pike-head and left him only the pole. He jumped down

---

*Patroclus (pə-trō'-kləs) *Ajax (ā'-jaks)
*Achilles (ə-kil'-ēz) *Hector (hek'-tēr)
*Myrmidon (mūr'-mi-dən)

and rejoined his comrades, who were holding the nearest row of huts. This allowed the Trojans to set the ship on fire. As soon as Achilles saw a thin column of smoke rising into the sky, he lent Patroclus his magnificent arms and armour, paraded the Myrmidons, and sent them forward to save the fleet. Their charge was irresistible. Mistaking Patroclus for Achilles, the Trojans were again driven out, and lost heavily.

Almighty Zeus, watching from Mount Ida, could not at first decide whether Patroclus should be immediately destroyed by Hector and stripped of Achilles's armour, or whether he should be granted fresh victories. In the end, Zeus let him go on for another half hour. Patroclus forgot his promise to Achilles as he chased the fleeing Trojans across the plain. A company of Myrmidons were already scaling the walls of Troy when Apollo showed himself on the Citadel* and shook his terrible shield at them. They retired in awe.

Hector then challenged Patroclus to a duel. No sooner had they dismounted from their chariots than Apollo stepped quietly behind Patroclus and struck him on the neck with the edge of his palm. Achilles's helmet tumbled off, Achilles's tough spear shattered, Achilles's shield slipped to the ground, and Patroclus stood there unarmed, dazed and trembling. Darting up, Hector speared him low in the belly; and the Trojans rallied when they saw him fall.

A fearful tussle followed for the body. Both Greeks and Trojans treated it like a newly-flayed bull's hide, which farm-boys tug in all directions, to stretch and

---

*Citadel (sit'-ə-d'l)

supple it. At last Menelaus and the Greeks succeeded in carrying the body back to camp, while Great and Little Ajax acted as rear-guards.

One of Nestor's* sons brought the bad news to Achilles, tears blinding his eyes. Achilles's two horses, Xanthus* and Balius,* which Patroclus had been driving, wept too—huge tears trickled down their noses. But he already knew. Hera had sent a message by Iris, and ordered him to stand on the rampart as soon as the Trojans, who were pursuing the retreating Greeks, appeared, and roar out a challenge. This would make them recoil in terror because, having watched Hector strip Achilles's well-known armour from Patroclus, they thought him dead. Achilles shouted so loud, and the Trojans halted in such confusion, that forty of them were wounded by the spears of men following behind, or run over by chariots.

Achilles wept, laid his enormous hands on Patroclus's bloody chest, howling horribly, like a lioness whose cub has been killed, and mourned all night long.

Thetis then persuaded Hephaestus, the lame Smith-god, to forge her son a new set of divine arms and armour. Hephaestus began his work immediately: ornamenting the shield with town and country scenes designed in silver, gold and precious stones. At dawn, Thetis brought her splendid gift to Achilles's hut. He put it on delightedly and was soon making a speech at a General Assembly.

'King Agamemnon,' he said, 'neither of us has profited in the least from our recent unfortunate quarrel about my slave-girl. The results have been so bad for you and

*Nestor (nes'-tēr)   *Balius (bal'-i-əs)
*Xanthus (zan'-thəs)

me that I almost wish she'd never been captured alive. Come, let bygones by bygones! And since your wounded arm still keeps you out of battle, why not make me temporary Commander-in-Chief?'

Agamemnon agreed. He even admitted his unfair treatment of Achilles, though blaming it on the Fates and a dark Fury called Mischief who, together, had robbed him of his senses.

When Achilles asked permission to advance at once, Agamemnon answered: 'I fear I can't grant you that favour. The men haven't yet breakfasted. But while their food is being got ready, I'll send servants to my storehut, and have all the treasures fetched that I recently offered you.'

'I want no treasures,' shouted Achilles, 'and the mere thought of breakfast nauseates me, with so many dead strewing the field!'

Nevertheless, Agamemnon's servants brought him the gold ingots, the tripods, the cauldrons, the slave-girls—including Briseis*—and the race-horses. Briseis flung herself on Patroclus's corpse, wailing loudly and praising his gentle, generous nature. 'He had always promised,' she sobbed, 'that Prince Achilles and I would be married in Greece, as soon as Troy fell.' Achilles, it seems, had kept his love of Polyxena,* daughter of Priam of Troy, a secret even from Patroclus.

He still refused to eat, but Athene gave him divine nourishment by smearing nectar and ambrosia on his skin, which made him feel enormously strong. Both armies then poured into the plain, where Almighty Zeus varied the day's battle by letting all the gods and god-

*Briseis (brī-sē'-is)
*Polyxena (pə-lik'-sə-nə)

desses take part, and fight one another if they pleased. There were five on each side. For the Greeks: Hera, Athene, Poseidon, Hermes the Herald, and Hephaestus the Smith. For the Trojans: Ares the War-god, Apollo, his sister Artemis the Huntress, his mother the Goddess Leto,* and the River-god Scamander.*

When the lines of battle clashed, Apollo kept Achilles from meeting Hector. He went to the Trojan hero, Aeneas,* in disguise and reminded him of his boast at a recent banquet:—'I'm ready to challenge the bravest of the Greeks—even Prince Achilles!'

Aeneas answered: 'That's very true. The last time we met I was unarmed, and a neutral—I had to run for my life. Besides, Athene was helping him, and no wise man opposes the gods.'

Apollo inspired him with courage. 'You also are under divine protection, Aeneas,' he said, 'and far better born than Achilles. His mother Thetis is an unimportant Sea-goddess: your mother is Aphrodite, a respected member of Zeus's Olympian Council.'

So Aeneas challenged Achilles, who only jeered at him, asking: 'Are you out to win King Priam's favour and get named as his successor? Why fool yourself?' When Aeneas did not reply, he went on: 'Priam still has several sons of his own. He'd never prefer a cousin to a son. Take my advice: retire unhurt!' 'And you, I suppose, fancy yourself as Agamemnon's successor?' Aeneas shouted, stung to anger.

Achilles found equally unkind things to say in return, but at last Aeneas, somehow controlling his temper, said: 'Why are we standing about and arguing like little boys?

*Leto (lē'-tō)   *Aeneas (i-nē'-əs)
*Scamander (skə-man'-dēr)

Words are cheap, so are insults. If we had time to spare, we could exchange enough of them to fill a two-hundred-oar galley. I came here to fight, not to gossip. Guard your head!'

The spear, flung with all his strength, made no dint in the wonderful shield that Hephaestus had forged; whereas Achilles's spear drove clean through the top of Aeneas's shield, burying itself in the ground behind him. Aeneas picked up a huge rock which, if he had thrown it, must merely have bounced back from the divine armour. Yet Poseidon knew that Almighty Zeus would be enraged if Aeneas, whose life he had decided to spare for his own best reasons, were to die. So he shrouded Achilles's eyes in a magical mist, and swung Aeneas high above the battlefield; laying him down beyond the Trojan lines, where his arrival greatly surprised some allied troops who were late in arming themselves. Achilles, no less surprised to find him vanished, shrugged his shoulders and went in search of Hector. He caught sight of twelve-year-old Polydorus,* King Priam's youngest and favourite son. The boy, despite strict orders to avoid danger, was dodging between the front row of fighters. Achilles transfixed his body with a javelin. Though Hector had been warned by Apollo to avoid Achilles's rage, the death of his little brother so infuriated him that he ran up, vengefully shaking a long spear.

'We meet at last!' cried Achilles.

Hector threw the spear, but a gust of wind sent by Athene made it curve back and fall at his feet. When Achilles rushed forward yelling vengeance, Apollo shrouded Hector in another thick mist. Three times

*Polydorus (pol'-i-dôr'-əs)

Achilles vainly charged at his invisible enemy, then turned his anger against lesser Trojans, roaring on like a forest fire as they broke and fled towards the Scamander. There, in the shallows and in hollows under the river banks, he massacred hundreds of them. The angry River-god Scamander appeared in human shape, crying 'Begone!' Achilles furiously sprang into mid-stream and yelled a challenge. Scamander gathered a great head of water and brought it rushing at Achilles, who braced himself by clutching at an elm-tree. This was soon uprooted, but he scrambled ashore, chased by Scamander in the form of a towering green wave. He would have drowned like a rat, had not Poseidon and Athene dragged him away, each holding a hand.

Scamander and his partner, the River-god Simoeis,* together pursued Achilles as he hurried off, but Hera ordered her son Hephaestus to oppose them. He kindled a fierce blaze on the plain, which burned the elms, willows, tamarisks, rushes and sedge of the river bank. Scamander's water soon boiled with such furious heat, that he appealed to Hera in pain and terror. 'Please recall your son!' he pleaded. 'I'll promise never to help Troy again.' Hera did as he asked, and Achilles continued his slaughter of Trojans.

Some other gods and goddesses had already come to blows. Ares attacked Athene, but his spear proved useless against the shield lent her by Almighty Zeus, and, throwing a huge black boundary-stone at his head, she knocked him flat. Ares's fallen body covered seven acres of land. Aphrodite was helping him to his feet, when

*Simoeis (sim'-ō-is)

Athene, at Hera's orders, felled her with a tremendous slap on the chest.

Hermes would not fight against the Goddess Leto, mother of Apollo and Artemis. He replied politely to her invitation: 'Madam, the victory is already yours.' Poseidon then challenged Apollo to a single combat, which he also refused. 'Why should we Gods injure each other for the sake of a few wretched mortals?' he asked calmly. Artemis the Huntress screamed at her brother, calling him a pitiful coward, but Hera rushed up, seized both of Artemis's wrists in one hand, snatched bow and arrows from her, and soundly boxed her ears.

Achilles meanwhile drove the Trojans headlong towards Troy, where Priam opened all the gates to admit them. Hector alone stood fast, in defence of the Western gateway. Priam wept and tore his white hair, begging him to come inside quickly, before he was shut out. Hector would not listen and, as Achilles rushed to the attack, turned and ran at great speed around the walls, hoping that the Trojans would drop heavy stones on his pursuer from the battlements. Achilles, however, followed too close behind to make this possible. The pair circled Troy four times. At last Athene, disguised as Hector's brother, Prince Deiphobus,* appeared beside him, yelling: 'Stop, Hector! Let us meet Achilles together, two against one!'

Deceived by the Goddess, he halted, faced about, and said sadly: 'Achilles, since this is a death-duel, you and I should swear that whoever kills and strips the other, will send the corpse to his people for decent burial.'

*Deiphobus (de-if'-ə-bəs)

Achilles's only reply was the whiz of a spear. Hector ducked, and hurled his own, which bounced harmlessly from the divine shield. He called over his shoulder: 'Quick, Deiphobus, lend me yours!' Getting no answer, Hector realized that Athene was tricking him. He drew his broadsword and charged. Athene had meanwhile invisibly restored Achilles's spear to him. Taking aim at Hector's bare neck, he sent his enemy crashing down.

'Spare my corpse,' Hector whispered. 'King Priam will ransom it at a noble price.' 'Scoundrel!' shouted Achilles. 'For the injury you've done me, I'll let the crows pick out your eyes and the dogs crunch your bones.'

So Hector died. Achilles stripped his body naked, then cut slits behind his heel-tendons, pulled Ajax's embroidered belt through them, buckled it to the tailboard of his chariot, lashed the team on, and dragged Hector after him, round and round the walls of Troy. Priam, Hecuba and Hector's widow, Andromache,* all watched horror-stricken from above.

Back in the camp, Achilles built a hundred-foot-square pyre for Patroclus's corpse, and there sacrificed a huge flock of sheep to his ghost; also four horses, nine hounds, and twelve noble Trojan prisoners of war, whom he had reserved for this fate. The blaze lit up many miles of the countryside. Next day he held funeral games in Patroclus's honour: a chariot race, a boxing bout, a wrestling match, a foot race and a javelin-throwing competition, all with valuable prizes. Still crazed by grief, he would rise every dawn to drag Hector's corpse three times round Patroclus's tomb. Apollo, however, tenderly protected it from decay or mutilation.

*Andromache (an-drom'-ə-ki)

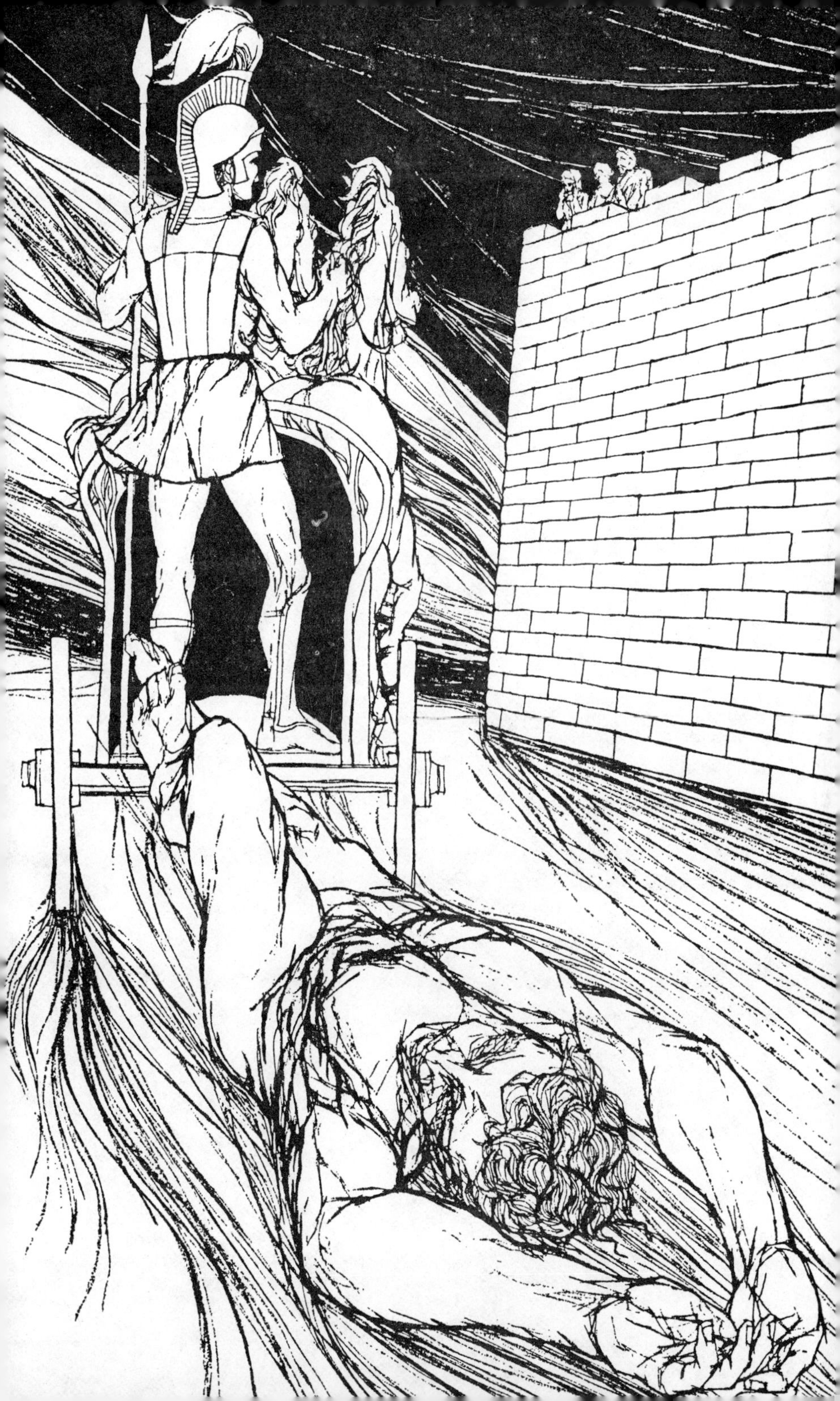

At last the God Hermes led King Priam to Achilles's hut under cover of darkness, and commanded Achilles to accept a fair ransom: the corpse's weight in pure gold. Priam loathed having to clasp his enemy's knees and kiss the terrible hands that had murdered so many of his sons, but forced himself to undergo this shame. Achilles treated him courteously, and even praised his courage in entering the enemy camp at night. They agreed on the ransom. However, by now so little gold remained in Priam's treasury, that when they presently met in the temple of Apollo, Priam's daughter Polyxena had to tip down the scale with her necklace and bracelets.

Achilles, impressed by this sisterly kindness and still deeply in love, told Priam: 'I'll cheerfully exchange your dead son for your living daughter. Keep this gold, marry her to me, and if you then return Helen to Menelaus, I'll arrange an honourable peace between our two peoples.'

Priam answered: 'No, take the gold, as we agreed, and let me have my son's body. But I'm ready to barter one live woman against another. Persuade your comrades to leave Helen at Troy, and I'll ask no marriage fee for Polyxena. We should be lost without Helen.'

Achilles undertook to do his best.

TALKING ABOUT THE STORY

1. Heroes emerge from every war.
    How did the Trojan warrior, Hector, display courage?

Could you tell that Patroclus had the interests of the Greeks at heart? Was he persuasive? forgetful? Explain.

Achilles's personality was a combination of kindness and cruelty—thought and impulse. How did he show tenderness? When was he heartless? thoughtful? impulsive? Which of these were his major qualities?

Which warrior did you admire most?

2. Gods and goddesses often affected the fortunes of war.

How did Apollo help Hector kill Patroclus? What message did Hera send Achilles after Hector killed Patroclus? What happened when Achilles followed Hera's advice?

The Olympians sometimes intervened in unique and amusing ways. Why did Apollo go to Aeneas in disguise? Why did Athene disguise herself as Prince Deiphobus? What important event next occurred? How did the gods use magical mists?

Can you remember other ways in which the gods meddled in the war?

3. Customs of a nation are revealed in stories about its people. What were some battle customs of the Greeks and Trojans? How did warriors express grief? How did they mourn the death of a friend? How did they celebrate triumph over a foe?

EXPRESSIONS FROM MYTHOLOGY

Suppose you heard that someone was "sulking like Achilles in his tent." Would you be able to explain how this expression originated?

GREEK WORDS IN OUR LANGUAGE

Chron is a Greek word meaning "time." A *chronicle* is a history. The story of the Trojan War is a *chronicle* of this war. The root *chron* is also found in many other words. How do people *synchronize* their watches? What is a *chronic* illness? a *chronological* list of events?

IDEAS FOR WRITING

1. If a Trojan boy and a Greek boy met on a remote part of the battlefield, what would they talk about? Who would be their favorite warriors? Which battle would they think was the most important? Would they argue about these points?
2. Suppose you are a member of a Greek or Trojan household, and your family is talking about the war—perhaps the death of Patroclus or Hector. Is your brother or father in the troops? What are the family's thoughts and feelings?

    Write a conversation that might take place in either of these situations.

Achilles scored triumph after triumph for the Greeks. If only he had kept an important secret, the hero might have continued to do great deeds.

the wooden horse

BY ROBERT GRAVES

The war dragged on. New allies came to King Priam's help, including the Amazon Queen Penthesileia* from Armenia, who killed King Machaon* and three times drove Achilles himself off the field. Finally, with Athene's help, Achilles ran her through. Memnon, the Negro King of Ethiopia, accounted for hundreds of Greeks, including Nestor's eldest son, and almost succeeded in burning the Greek ships; but Great Ajax challenged him to a duel, which was rudely interrupted by Achilles. He ran up, brushed Ajax aside, speared Memnon, and threw the Trojans back once more.

This proved to be Achilles's last victory, because when that night he met Polyxena by private arrangement in Apollo's temple, she wormed out of him his most important secret. Polyxena was sworn to avenge her beloved brother Hector, and there is nothing a beautiful

*Penthesileia (pen'-the-si-lē'-ə)
*Machaon (ma-kā'-on)

girl cannot make a man tell her as a proof of love. He revealed that when Thetis dipped him in Styx* water as a child, to make him invulnerable, she had tightly held his right heel, which stayed dry and unprotected.

They met again next day at the same place, to confirm his promise that, after marrying Polyxena, he would so arrange matters that the Greeks went home without Helen. King Priam had insisted on his offering a sacrifice to Apollo and taking an oath at the God's altar. Achilles came barefoot and unarmed; but two of Priam's sons, Deiphobus and Paris, whom Priam sent to represent him, were secretly plotting murder. Prince Deiphobus embraced Achilles, in pretence of friendship, while Paris, hiding behind a pillar, shot at his heel. The barbed arrow, guided by Aphrodite, wounded him mortally. Though Achilles snatched firebrands from the altar and struck vengefully at Paris and Deiphobus, they got away; and he killed a couple of temple servants only.

Odysseus* and Great Ajax, who suspected Achilles of treachery, had crept after him into the temple. Dying in their arms, he made them swear that when Troy fell they would sacrifice Polyxena at his tomb. Paris and Deiphobus returned to fetch the body; but Odysseus and Ajax beat them off in a stiff fight and brought it safely back.

Agamemnon, Menelaus and the rest of the Council shed tears at Achilles's funeral, though few ordinary soldiers regretted the death of so notorious a traitor. His ashes, mixed with those of Patroclus, were placed in a golden urn and buried in a lofty barrow at the entrance to the Hellespont.

*Styx (stiks)
*Odysseus (ō-dis′-ūs)

Thetis awarded Achilles's arms and armour to the bravest Greek leader left before Troy; and to embarrass Agamemnon, for whom she felt a deep scorn, appointed him the judge. Odysseus and Great Ajax, having successfully defended his corpse against the Trojans, came forward as rivals for this honour. But Agamemnon feared the anger of whoever lost so valuable a prize, and sent spies by night to listen under the walls of Troy and report what the Trojans themselves thought.

The spies crept up close, and after awhile a party of Trojan girls began to chat above them. One praised Ajax's courage in lifting Achilles's corpse on his shoulders and taking it through a shower of spears and arrows. Another said: 'Nonsense, Odysseus showed far greater courage! Even a slave-girl will do what Ajax did, if given a corpse to carry; but put weapons in her hand, and she'll never dare use them. Ajax used that corpse as a shield, while Odysseus kept our men off with spear and sword.'

On the strength of this report, Agamemnon awarded the arms to Odysseus. The Council knew that he would never have preferred him to Great Ajax if Achilles had been alive—Achilles thought the world of his gallant cousin. Besides,—the spies understood no Phrygian, and were probably prompted by Odysseus. Yet no one dared say so.

In a blind rage, Ajax swore revenge on Agamemnon, Menelaus, Odysseus, and their fellow-Councillors. That night Athene sent him mad and he ran howling, sword in hand, among the flocks he had captured in raids on Trojan farms. After immense butchery, he chained the surviving sheep and goats together, hauled them to camp, and went on with his bloody work. He chose two rams, cut out the tongue of the largest, which he mistook for Agamemnon, and lopped off its head. Then he tied the other to a pillar by the neck and flogged it unmercifully, screaming abuse and shouting: 'Take that, and that, and that, treacherous Odysseus!' At last, coming to his senses, and greatly ashamed of himself, he fixed the sword which Hector had given him upright in the ground, and leaped upon it. His last words were a prayer to the Furies for vengeance. Odysseus wisely avoided this danger by presenting the armour to Achilles's ten-year-old son Neoptolemus,* who had just joined the Greek forces and, like his father at the same age, was already full-grown.

Calchas prophesied that Troy could be taken only with the help of Heracles's bow and arrows, now owned by King Philoctetes.* Odysseus and Diomedes* sailed to fetch them from the small island off Lemnos where, nine years before, the Greeks had left the wounded Philoctetes marooned. Even after nine years, his wound smelt as badly as ever, nor had the pain grown less. Odysseus stole his bow and arrows by a trick; but Diomedes, not wishing to be mixed up in so dishonourable an affair, made him restore them, and persuaded Philoctetes to come aboard their ship. When they landed at Troy, Machaon's brother cured him with soothing herbs and a precious stone called serpentine.

No sooner was Philoctetes well again than he challenged Paris to an archery duel. Paris shot first, and aimed at his enemy's heart, but the arrow went wide— Athene, of course, saw to that. Philoctetes then let loose three arrows in quick succession. The first pierced Paris's bow-hand, the next his right eye, and the last his ankle.

*Neoptolemus (nē'-op-tol'-ə məs)   *Diomedes (dī'-ə-mē'-dēz)
*Philoctetes (fil'-ok-tē'-tēz)

He hobbled from the fight and, though Menelaus tried to catch and kill him, managed to reach Troy and die in Helen's arms.

Helen was now a widow, but King Priam could still not bear the idea of restoring her to Menelaus; and his sons wrangled among themselves, each wanting to be her husband. Helen then remembered that she had been Queen of Sparta and Menelaus's wife. One night a sentry caught her as she was about to climb down a rope from the battlements; whereupon Deiphobus married her by force—an act which disgusted the entire royal family.

Jealous quarrels between Priam's sons grew so fierce that he sent his warrior Antenor* to discuss peace terms with the Greeks. But Antenor had not forgiven Deiphobus for having helped Paris to murder Achilles in Apollo's own temple, a sacrilege which Priam left unpunished. Antenor told Agamemnon's Council that he would betray Troy if they made him King afterwards and gave him half the spoils. According to an ancient oracle, he said, Troy would not fall until the Palladium,* a legless wooden image of Athene, some four feet high, had been stolen from her temple on the Citadel. As it happened, the Greeks already knew of this prophecy through Helenus, Cassandra's twin brother, who was madly jealous of Deiphobus's marriage. So Antenor promised to hand over the Palladium when Athene's two favourites, Odysseus and Diomedes, had entered Troy by a secret way he would show them.

That night, Odysseus and Diomedes set out together and, following Antenor's instructions, cleared away a pile of stones under the western wall. They found that it hid the exit of a long, wide, dirty-water pipe leading

*Antenor (an-tē'-nor)   *Palladium (pə-lā'-di-əm)

straight up to the Citadel. Antenor's wife Theano,* warned what to expect, had drugged the temple servants; so that Diomedes and Odysseus met no trouble at all once they reached the top by a hard, filthy climb. To make sure that the servants were not shamming sleep, they cut their throats and then returned the same way. Theano lowered the Palladium down after them, and put a replica in its place.

Diomedes, being higher in rank, carried the Palladium strapped to his shoulders, but Odysseus, who wanted all the glory for himself, let him go ahead and then stealthily unsheathed his sword. The rising moon peered large and bright over a crest of Mount Ida, throwing the shadow of Odysseus's upraised sword-arm in front of Diomedes. He spun around, drew his own sword, disarmed Odysseus, tied his hands behind him, and drove him forward with repeated kicks and blows. Back in the Council Hut, Odysseus protested violently against Diomedes's treatment. He claimed to have unsheathed his sword because he heard a Trojan coming in pursuit. Agamemnon counted too much on Odysseus's help not to agree that Diomedes must have been mistaken.

Athene now inspired Odysseus to think of a stratagem for getting armed men into Troy. Under his directions, Epeius* the Phocian,* the best carpenter in camp though a fearful coward, built an enormous hollow horse out of fir planks. It had a concealed trap-door fitted into the left flank, and on the right a sentence carved in tall letters: 'With thankful hope of a safe return to their homes after nine years' absence, the Greeks dedicate this offering to Athene.' Odysseus entered the horse by means of a rope-ladder, followed by Menelaus, Diomedes, Achilles's

*Theano (thē'-ə-nō) *Phocian (fō-sē'-ən)
*Epeius (ē'-pi-əs)

son Neoptolemus, and by eighteen more volunteers. Coaxed, threatened and bribed, Epeius was forced to sit by the trap door, which he alone could open quickly and silently.

Having gathered all their gear together, the Greeks set fire to their huts, launched the ships, and rowed off; but no farther than the other side of Tenedos,* where they were invisible from Troy. Odysseus's companions already filled the horse, and only one Greek was left in the camp: his cousin Sinon.*

When Trojan scouts went out at dawn they found the horse towering over the burned camp. Antenor knew nothing about the horse and therefore kept quiet, but King Priam and several of his sons wanted to bring it into the city on rollers. Others shouted: 'Athene has favoured the Greeks far too long! Let her do what she pleases with her property.' Priam would listen neither to their protests nor to Aeneas's urgent warnings.

The horse had been purposely built too large for Troy's gates, and stuck four times even when these were removed and some stones pulled away from the wall on one side. With strenuous efforts the Trojans hauled it up to the Citadel, but at least took the precaution of rebuilding the wall and putting the gates back on their hinges. Priam's daughter Cassandra, whose curse was that no Trojan would ever take her prophecies seriously, screamed: 'Beware: the horse is full of armed men!'

Meanwhile two soldiers came across Sinon, hiding in a turret by the camp gate, and marched him to the Royal Palace. Asked why he had stayed behind, he told King Priam: 'I was afraid to sail in the same ship as my

*Tenedos (ten'-ə-dos)   *Sinon (sī'-nən)

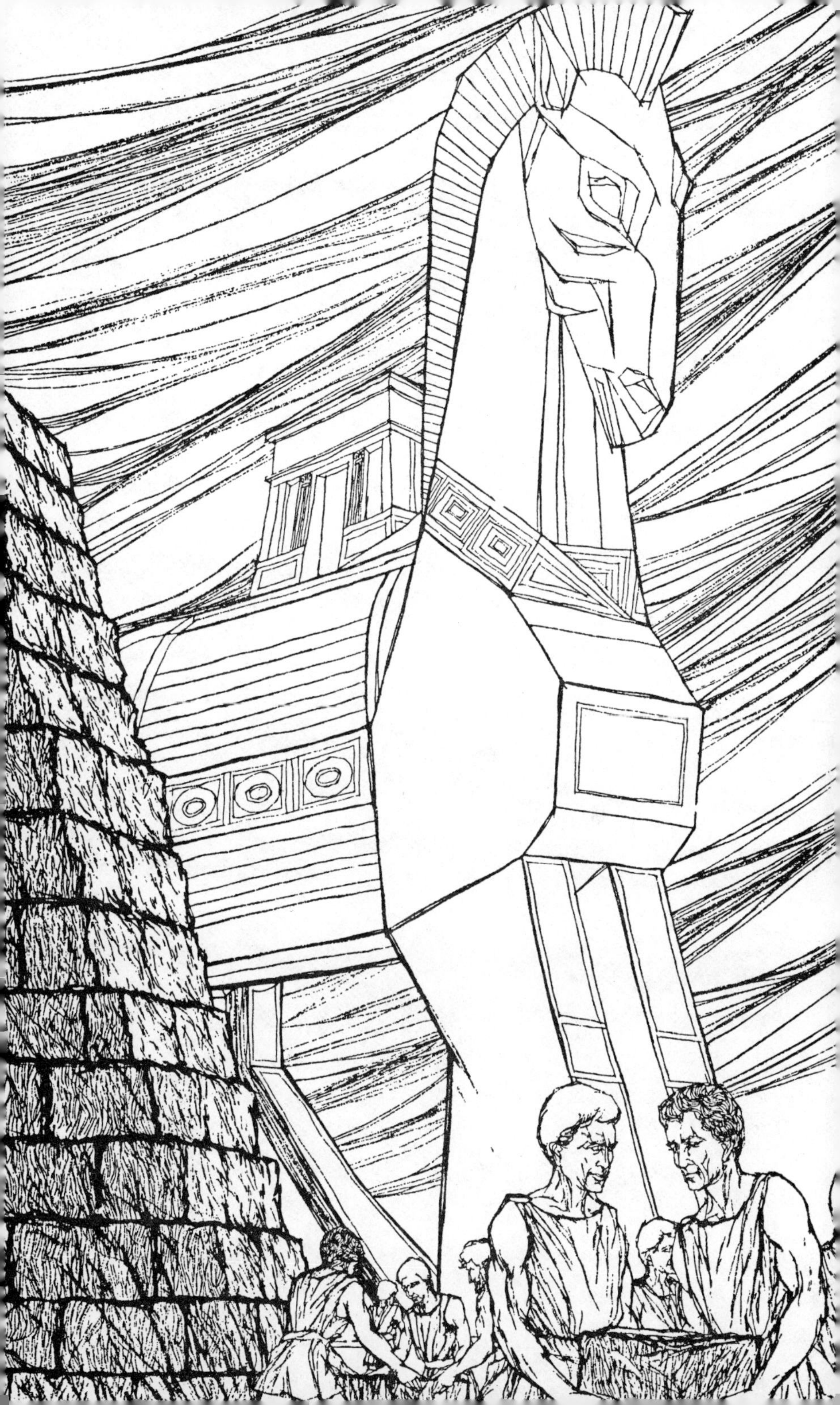

cousin Odysseus. He has long wanted to kill me, and yesterday nearly succeeded.'

'Why should Odysseus want to kill you?' asked Priam.

'Because I alone know how he got one of the Greeks stoned, and he doesn't trust my discretion. The fleet would have sailed a month ago, if the weather hadn't been so bad. Calchas of course prophesied, just as he did at Aulis, that a human sacrifice was needed, and Odysseus said: "Name the victim, please!" Calchas refused an immediate answer, but some days later (bribed, I suppose, by Odysseus) he named me. I was on the point of being sacrificed, when a favourable wind sprang up, I escaped in the excitement, and off they went.'

Priam believed Sinon's tale, freed him and asked for an explanation of the horse. Sinon answered: 'You remember those two temple servants who were found mysteriously murdered on the Citadel? That was Odysseus's work. He came by night, drugged the priestesses, and stole the Palladium. If you don't trust me, look carefully at what you think is the Palladium. You'll find that it's only a replica. Odysseus's theft made Athene so angry that the real Palladium, hidden in Agamemnon's hut, sweated as a warning of disaster. Calchas had a huge horse built in her honour. and warned Agamemnon to sail home.'

'Why was it made so huge?' asked Priam.

'To prevent it from being brought into the city. Calchas prophesied that if you succeeded in this, you could then raise an immense expedition from all over Asia Minor, invade Greece, and sack Agamemnon's own city of Mycenae.'

A Trojan nobleman named Laocoön* interrupted Sinon by shouting: 'My lord King, these are certainly lies put into Sinon's mouth by Odysseus. Otherwise Agamemnon would have left the Palladium behind as well as the horse.' He added: 'And by the way, my lord, may I suggest that we sacrifice a bull to Poseidon—whose priest you stoned nine years ago because he refused to welcome Queen Helen?'

'I don't agree with you about the horse,' said Priam. 'But now that the war has ended, let us by all means regain Poseidon's favour. He treated us cruelly enough while it lasted.'

Laocoön went off to build an altar near the camp, and chose a young and healthy bull for sacrifice. He was preparing to strike it down with his axe, when a couple of immense monsters crawled from the sea and, twining around Laocoön's limbs and those of the two sons who were helping him, crushed the life out of them. The monsters then glided up to the Citadel, and there bowed their heads in honour of Athene—a sight which Priam unfortunately took to mean that Sinon had told the truth, and that Laocoön had been killed for contradicting him. In fact, however, Poseidon sent the sea-beasts at Athene's request: as a proof that he hated the Trojans as much as she did.

Priam dedicated the horse to Athene and although Aeneas led his men safely away from Troy, suspecting any gift of the Greeks and refusing to believe the war ended—everyone else began victory celebrations. Trojan women visited the Scamander for the first time in nine years, gathering flowers by its banks to decorate the

*Laocoön (lā-ok'-ə-won')

horse's wooden mane. They also spread a carpet of roses around its hooves. A tremendous banquet was got ready at Priam's palace.

Meanwhile, inside the horse, few of the Greeks could stop trembling. Epeius wept silently in utter terror, but Odysseus held a sword against his ribs, and if he had heard so much as a sigh would have driven it home. That evening, Helen strolled along and took a closer look at the horse. She reached up to pat its flanks and, as though to amuse Deiphobus who came with her, teased the hidden occupants by mimicking the voices of all their wives in turn. Not being a Trojan, she knew that Cassandra always spoke the truth; and also guessed which of the Greek leaders would have volunteered for this dangerous task. Diomedes and two others were tempted to answer 'Here I am!' when they heard their names spoken, but Odysseus restrained them and even had to strangle one man in the process.

Worn out by drinking and dancing, the Trojans slept soundly, and not even the bark of a dog broke the stillness. Helen alone lay awake, listening. At midnight, just before the full moon rose, the seventh of the year, Sinon crept from the city to light a beacon on Achilles's tomb; and Antenor waved a torch from the battlements. Agamemnon, whose ship lay anchored close offshore, replied to these signals by lighting a brazier filled with chips of pinewood. The whole fleet then quietly landed.

Antenor, tip-toeing up to the wooden horse, said in low tones: 'All's well! You may come out.' Epeius unlocked the trap door so noiselessly that someone fell through and broke his neck. The rest climbed down the rope-ladder. Two men went to open the City gates for Agamemnon; others murdered the sleeping sentries. But Menelaus could think only of Helen and, followed by Odysseus, ran at full speed towards Deiphobus's house.

epilogue

Troy was chaotic for three days and three nights. The Greeks ransacked homes, murdered people in their sleep, and set the town ablaze.

King Priam, Queen Hecuba, and Polyxena sought refuge at the altar of Zeus. There Neoptolemus, Achilles's son, slaughtered Priam.

Meanwhile, Menelaus and Odysseus reached Deiphobus's house. While Deiphobus was trying to kill the two Greeks, Helen stabbed him in the back.

According to Achilles's request, Polyxena was sacrificed at his tomb. Agamemnon took Cassandra as a prize of war and Neoptolemus took Andromache, Hector's widow, as his slave.

Aeneas and Antenor were the only Trojan heroes to survive the war. Aeneas had seen the flames of Troy and had fled to Thrace during the three-day siege. Antenor didn't become King of Troy, nor did he receive part of the spoils. Antenor, Theano, and their four sons sailed away in Menelaus's ship and founded cities in lands which are now North Africa and Italy.

Odysseus had planned to enslave Hecuba, but she shrieked so horribly that he decided to kill her. Hecuba escaped death by turning herself into a ferocious black dog whose howling terrified everyone. The gods forced Odysseus to wander for ten years before he returned home to Ithaca.

When Diomedes returned to Argos, he found that another man now reigned as king. So Diomedes went to Italy where he founded the city of Brindisi.

Athene delayed Menelaus's and Helen's homecoming because they had not offered sacrifices to her. They finally reached Sparta after having been away for eighteen years.

Nestor was the only Greek who had a joyful reception at home. He spent the rest of his days telling tales about the war.

TALKING ABOUT THE STORY

1. The Greek warriors were proud and independent leaders. As the war dragged on, distrust, quarrels, and misunderstandings arose among them. How did jealousy create dissension between Agamemnon and Achilles? between Ajax and Odysseus?
2. The interaction of personalities resulted in several difficult situations.

    Many of the Greek soldiers thought Achilles was a traitor. How had he acted when Patroclus begged him to fight? What bargain had he made with King Priam? What secret had Polyxena wormed out of him?

    Describe Agamemnon's personality. How did he explain his harsh treatment of Achilles? Why did Agamemnon award the armor to Odysseus?

Did Odysseus employ his ingenuity during the Trojan war? How? Was he ruthless as well? When?

3. Do you think the Trojans ever suspected that Antenor was a traitor? What made him turn against the Trojans? How did he help the Greeks?

4. The gods contributed to the deaths of several heroes. How did Paris's arrow reach Achilles's heel? Why did Ajax commit suicide? Would Philoctetes have shot Paris if Athena hadn't interfered?

5. Apollo ensured that no one would ever heed Cassandra's prophecies. Suppose people had listened to Cassandra. What might have happened? Did the outcome of the war depend upon any other prophecies?

6. Conspiracy was important in the defeat of Troy. Why did the Greeks pretend to leave the shores of Troy? How did Sinon deceive the Trojans?

7. Have you ever seen a petty quarrel mushroom into a serious argument? In the Trojan War stories, a jealous spat grew into a chain reaction of vengeful deeds. After the beauty contest Hera and Athene stormed away, vowing to ruin Troy. Why? What acts of revenge followed?

EXPRESSIONS FROM MYTHOLOGY

1. Whose face "launch'd a thousand ships"? Explain.
2. Achilles's heel was his one vulnerable spot. If you heard someone speak of a person's "Achilles's heel," what would he mean?

3. Cassandra's name can be found today in the expression "a Cassandran utterance." Why is this phrase a fitting description for words that fall on deaf ears?
4. The Trojans tried very hard to save their city. If you read that someone worked "like a Trojan," what would you know about the way he tackled assignments?
5. Throughout history men have been warned to "beware of a Trojan Horse." If someone called a gift a "Trojan Horse," what would he mean?

IDEAS FOR WRITING

It is the night of the fall of Troy. The wooden horse is within the walls. Imagine that you are:

Cassandra and no one will heed your warnings. Which warriors do you talk to? How do you try to convince them to listen?

Odysseus inside the horse. Are you afraid the men will make noise? Do you have shrewd plans for killing various Trojans?

Helen waiting for reunion with the Greeks. How do you feel about returning to Sparta?

You keep a diary. Record your thoughts during the two hours before the trap door is opened.

GLOSSARY

Achilles (ə-kil′-ēz): Greek hero of the Trojan War. His only vulnerable spot was his heel.

Aegeus (ē′-joos): father of Theseus. He drowned himself because he thought the Minotaur had killed Theseus.

Aeneas (i-nē′-əs): hero and defender of Troy; founded Rome.

Agamemnon (ag′-ə-mem′-nən): commander of Greek army in Trojan War.

Ajax (ā′-jaks): fleet-footed Greek hero in Trojan War.

Alcyone (al-sī′-ə-ni): wife of Ceyx.

Amazons (am′-ə-zons′): female warriors. Hercules subdued their queen.

Antenor (an-tē′-nor): one of Priam's sons; a Trojan traitor.

Aphrodite (af′-rə-di′-ti): Greek Goddess of Love and Beauty. Roman name Venus.

Apollo (ə-pol′-ō): Greek God of Sunlight, Music, Poetry, Medicine; sometimes called Phoebus or Phoebus Apollo. Roman name the same.

Arachne (ə-rak′-ni): a mortal woman who challenged Athena to a weaving contest.

Ares (âr′-ēz): Greek God of War. Roman name Mars.

Argo (är′-gō): the ship of Jason and the Argonauts.

Ariadne (ar′-i-ad′-ni): daughter of Minos. She aided Theseus.

Artemis (är′-tə-mis): Greek Goddess of Hunting and the Moon. Roman name Diana.

Athena, Athene (ə-thē′-nə): Greek Goddess of Wisdom, Women's Handicrafts, and Battle; also called Pallas and Pallas Athena. Roman name Minerva.

Atlas (at′-ləs): a Titan. He carried the world on his shoulders.

Briseis (brī-sē′-is): a slave-girl of Achilles, taken away by Agamemnon.

Calchas (kal′-kəs): one of Apollo's priests in the Greek army at Troy.

Cassandra (kə-san′-drə): prophetess whom no Trojan believed.

centaur (sen′-tôr): a creature half-man, half-horse who lived in the mountains of Thessaly.

Cerberus (sûr′-bēr-əs): three-headed dog that guarded the entrance to the underworld.

Ceres (sêr′-ēz): Roman name for Demeter.

Ceyx (sē′-iks): husband of Alcyone. Zeus turned the two into sea-birds.

Chiron (kī′-ron): centaur who taught Jason and Hercules.

Clytie (klī′-ti): a nymph who loved Apollo. The gods turned her into a sunflower.

Cyclopes (sī′-klō-pēz): race of giants who had one eye in the center of their foreheads.

Daedalos (ded′-ə-ləs): builder of the Cretan labyrinth and inventor of wax wings.

Daphne (daf′-ni): a nymph whose father changed her into a laurel tree.
Deiphobus (dē-if′-ə-bəs): a Trojan hero; son of Priam.
Demeter (di-mē′-tēr): Greek Goddess of Agriculture; Roman name Ceres.
Diana (dī-an′-ə): Roman name for Artemis.
Eris (ēr′-is): Greek Goddess of Quarrels and Discord.
Eurystheus (yōō-ris′-thūs): king of Mycenae. He assigned Hercules the twelve labors.
Fates, three (fātz): Clotho, Lachesis, Atropos; goddesses who spun, measured, and cut the thread of life.
Fury (fyoor′-i): one of the avenging goddesses.
Gorgons (gôr′-gənz): the three dragon-sisters who turned men into stone.
Hades (hā′-dēz): the underworld. Greek name for Pluto.
Hecate (hek′-ə-ti): Greek Goddess of Moon, Earth, Realm of the Dead, Sorcery and Witchcraft.
Hector (hek′-tēr): Trojan warrior; son of Priam; killed in Trojan War by Achilles.
Hecuba (hek′-yoo-bə): wife of Priam.
Helenus (hel′-ə-nəs): a prophet no Trojan could believe; Cassandra's twin brother.
Hephaestus (hi-fes′-təs): Greek God of Metalwork and Fire.
Hera (hêr′-ə): wife of Zeus. Queen of the gods and goddesses. Roman name Juno.
Hercules (hūr′-kyōō-lēz′): hero who accomplished the twelve labors assigned by Eurystheus. Roman name for Heracles.
Hermes (hūr′-mēz): Greek God of Thieves and Heralds: Messenger of the Gods. Roman name Mercury.
Hesione (he-sī′-ə-ni): sister of Priam.
Hestia (hes′-ti-ə): Greek Goddess of the Hearth. Roman name Vesta.
Icaros (i′-kə-rəs): Daedalos's son who flew too close to the sun and burned.
Jason (jā′-s'n): the Greek prince who led the Argonauts on the quest for the Golden Fleece.
Juno (jōō′-nō): Roman name for Hera.
Jupiter (jōō′-pə-tēr): Roman name for Zeus.
Lethe (lē′-thi): river in the underworld; drinking its water caused complete forgetfulness.
Mars (märz): Roman name for Ares.
Medea (mi-dē′-ə): daughter of Aeetes. She helped Jason obtain the Golden Fleece.
Medusa (mə-dōō′-sə): the gorgon Perseus killed.
Menelaus (men-ə-lā′-əs): king of Sparta, Greece; husband of Helen.
Mercury (mur′-kyoo-ri): Roman name for Hermes.
Minerva (mi-nūr′-və): Roman name for Athena.

Minos (mī'-nəs): king of Crete. He had the labyrinth built as a pen for the Minotaur.

Minotaur (min'-ə-tôr'): Cretan monster with a bull's head and a man's body.

Morpheus (môr'-fi-əs): the God of Dreams; son of Somnus, the God of Sleep.

Narcissus (när-sis'-əs): a youth who fell in love with his reflection in a pool.

Neoptolemus (nē'-op-tol'-ə-məs): son of Achilles; slew Priam.

Nestor (nes'-tēr): Greek warrior; counseled the Greeks wisely in the Trojan War.

nymphs (nimfs): nature goddesses who lived in trees, glens, rivers, and the sea.

Odysseus (ō-dis'-ūs): Greek warrior known for cleverness.

Palladium (pə-lā'-di-əm): wooden statue of Pallas Athena, on whose preservation the safety of Troy depended.

Pandora (pan-dôr'-ə): the first woman. She let troubles into the world.

Paris (par'-is): son of Priam. He kidnapped and married Helen.

Patroclus (pə-trō'-cləs): Greek hero slain by Hector and avenged by Achilles.

Perseus (pūr'-sūs): Greek hero who slew Medusa.

Phaethon (fā'-ə-t'n): son of Apollo. He drove Apollo's chariot too close to the earth.

Philoctetes (fil'-ok-tē'-tēz): Greek warrior who killed Paris in the Trojan War.

Polydorus (pol'-i-dôr'-əs): youngest son of Priam. Achilles killed him.

Polyphemus (pol'-i-fē'-məs): the Cyclops blinded by Odysseus.

Polyxena (pə-lik'-sə-nə): daughter of Priam and Hecuba. Achilles loved her.

Priam (prī'-am): king of Troy.

Prometheus (prə-mē'-thūs): a Titan who gave man fire.

Proserpina (prō-sŭr'-pi-nə): daughter of Ceres and Jupiter; kidnapped by Pluto. Greek name Persephone.

Quicksilver (kwik'-sil'-vēr): another name for Hermes; Mercury.

satyr (sat'-ēr): woodland god with the ears of a horse, body of a man, and legs of a goat.

Somnus (som'-nəs): Greek god of Sleep.

Styx (stiks): one of the rivers which separated the underworld from the world above.

Theseus (thē'-sōōs): hero of Athens; killed the Minotaur.

Thetis (thē'-tis): a Nereid; mother of Achilles.

Titans (tī'-tənz): giant gods who ruled the world until Zeus overthrew them.

Venus (vē'-nəs): Roman name for Aphrodite.

Vesta (ves'-tə): Roman name for Hestia.

Vulcan (vul'-kən): Roman name for Hephaestus.

Zeus (zōōs): king of the Greek gods and goddesses. Roman name Jupiter.